ABRAHAM
THE FRIEND OF GOD

BIBLE STUDY GUIDE

From the Bible-teaching ministry of

Charles R. Swindoll

INSIGHT FOR LIVING

Charles R. Swindoll is a graduate of Dallas Theological Seminary and has served in pastorates for more than twenty-five years, including churches in Texas, New England, and California. Since 1971 he has served as senior pastor of the First Evangelical Free Church of Fullerton, California. Chuck's radio program, "Insight for Living," began in 1979. In addition to his church and radio ministries, Chuck enjoys writing. He has authored numerous books and booklets on a variety of subjects.

Based on the outlines of Chuck's sermons, the study guide text was coauthored by David Lien, a graduate of Westmont College and Dallas Theological Seminary. The Living Insights are written by Bill Butterworth, a graduate of Florida Bible College, Dallas Theological Seminary, and Florida Atlantic University. David Lien is presently the director of counseling ministries at Insight for Living, and Bill Butterworth is currently a staff writer in the Educational Products Department.

Editor in Chief:
Cynthia Swindoll
Coauthor of Text:
David Lien
Author of Living Insights:
Bill Butterworth
Editorial Assistant:
Glenda Schlahta
Copy Manager:
Jac La Tour
Copy Editor:
Connie Laser
Director, Communications Division:
Carla Beck

Project Manager:
Nina Paris
Project Supervisor:
Cassandra Clark
Designer:
Steve Cox
Production Artists:
Steve Cox and Diana Vasquez
Typographer:
Bob Haskins
Print Production Manager:
Deedee Snyder
Printer:
Frye and Smith

Unless otherwise identified, all Scripture references are from the New American Standard Bible, © The Lockman Foundation 1960, 1962, 1963, 1968, 1971, 1972, 1973, 1975, 1977. Used by permission.

ISBN 0-8499-8239-0

COVER PAINTING: Jan I. Lievens's, *Abraham's Offering*, from SuperStock International, Inc.

Table of Contents

Abraham . . . The Friend of God

When we think of a list of biblical characters who belong among "God's greatest," Abraham would certainly be included. He towers among many as a man of incredible faith. At a time when we are running shy of heroes, it is reassuring to know that a man of Abraham's caliber is portrayed so clearly in Scripture.

As you study his life, I'd like to suggest a couple of practical ways to transfer the traits that made Abraham great into your own life. First, as you read each lesson, think of Abraham as a real human being . . . not a super-saint or some unparalleled giant who lived an unachievable life. The longer you keep him on a pedestal, the less you'll be stimulated to emulate his model. Second, each time you hear a principle that motivates you to handle your world the same way Abraham did, put it into action right away! You may be amazed to discover, firsthand, that God's truth works as beautifully today as it did in the days of the patriarchs.

I'll be praying that the life of Abraham will help you translate theoretical faith in print to realistic faith in your life. As that occurs, let's be sure God gets the glory.

Chuck Swindoll

Putting Truth into Action

Knowledge apart from application falls short of God's desire for His children. Knowledge must result in change and growth. Consequently, we have constructed this Bible study guide with these purposes in mind: (1) to stimulate discovery, (2) to increase understanding, and (3) to encourage application.

At the end of each lesson is a section called 📖 *Living Insights*. There you'll be given assistance in further Bible study, and you'll be encouraged to contemplate and apply the things you've learned. This is the place where the lesson is fitted with shoe leather for your walk through the varied experiences of life.

In wrapping up some lessons, you'll find a unit called ⚒ *Digging Deeper*. It will provide you with essential information and list helpful resource materials so that you can probe further into some of the issues raised in those studies.

It's our hope that you'll discover numerous ways to use this tool. Some useful avenues we suggest are personal meditation, joint discovery, and discussion with your spouse, family, work associates, friends, or neighbors. The study guide is also practical for Sunday school classes, Bible study groups, and, of course, as a study aid for the "Insight for Living" radio broadcast.

In order to derive the greatest benefit from this process, we suggest that you record your responses to the lessons in the space which has been provided for you. In view of the kinds of questions asked, your study guide may become a journal filled with your many discoveries and commitments. We anticipate that you will find yourself returning to it periodically for review and encouragement.

David Lien
Coauthor of Text

Bill Butterworth
Author of Living Insights

ABRAHAM
THE FRIEND OF GOD

The Man Who Pioneered Faith

Genesis 11–13, 15, 17–18, 21–22, 25

Pioneers are a breed apart. They are the folks who dare to poke and probe in uncharted territory, while others nudge and nod from a safe but sterile distance.

Take the founders of space travel, for example. Three innovative men, each unaware of the others, launched our world into an unexpected new era. In 1903, the Russian Konstantin E. Tsiolkovsky first speculated that a rocket could travel beyond the earth's atmosphere. Herman Oberth, a Transylvanian-German, developed the first mathematical model for space travel in 1923. And in 1926, Robert H. Goddard, from a farm near Auburn, Massachusetts, launched the first liquid-propellant rocket.

Few comprehended the impact these men would make, yet our world has been forever changed by their unquenchable pioneer spirit.

Abraham, too, was a pioneer. Instead of spacecraft, it was *faith* that he took into uncharted territory, experiencing an adventure with God that has been retold through the centuries—and his story has never ceased to ignite human hearts.

I. Faith Is Simple

Christianity is not complicated; it's neglecting Christ that causes complication. Let's take a look at some people who show us the secrets of simple faith.

A. In the first century. The apostle Paul's faith reflected simplicity, as seen in the parallel he draws.

As you therefore have received Christ Jesus the Lord, so walk in Him. (Col. 2:6)

The way you first trusted Christ is precisely the way you walk with Him ... by faith.

B. In the fifteenth century. Thomas à Kempis, an Augustinian monk, felt that simplicity and purity are the measures of a person's walk with God.

1

Simplicity ought to be in our intention; purity in our affection. Simplicity tends toward God; purity apprehends and tastes Him.[1]

Simplicity comes when we become motivated by a single, mastering Life within us. Such resolve of purpose causes us to see life as God intended, and His purposes become our own (Ps. 37:3).

C. In the twentieth century. Anne Morrow Lindbergh, widow of the famed pilot Charles Lindbergh, sought simplicity. Perhaps her words echo some thoughts you have had:

I want first of all ... to be at peace with myself. I want a singleness of eye, a purity of intention, a central core to my life that will enable me to carry out these obligations and activities as well as I can. ... I would like to achieve a state of inner spiritual grace from which I could function and give as I was meant to in the eye of God. ... I have learned by some experience, by many examples, and by the writings of countless others before me ... that certain environments, certain modes of life, certain rules of conduct are more conducive to inner and outer harmony than others. There are, in fact, certain roads that one may follow. Simplification of life is one of them.[2]

All of these explorers of the godly life exhibited lives of simple faith ... a removal of striving, a refusal to be several selves, a determination to maintain the central core of their person in all simplicity.

II. Faith Gives Us New Frontiers (Genesis 11:26–12:4)

Pioneers come from the same human stock we do. Every one of us has a hometown, parents, and choices to make in life. Abram—later called Abraham—was no different. He was born to Terah, had two brothers, was raised in the city of Ur, and married Sarai. Abram's life was like anyone else's, but with two complications: his wife was unable to have children, and God told him to leave his hometown.

A. God redirects Abram's roots.

Now the Lord said to Abram,
"Go forth from your country,
And from your relatives
And from your father's house,
To the land which I will show you;
And I will make you a great nation,

---

1. Thomas à Kempis, *The Imitation of Christ* (Chicago, Ill.: Moody Press, n.d.), p. 69.

2. Anne Morrow Lindbergh, *Gift from the Sea* (New York, N.Y.: Random House, Vintage Books, 1955), pp. 23–24.

And I will bless you,
And make your name great;
And so you shall be a blessing;
And I will bless those who bless you,
And the one who curses you I will curse.
And in you all the families of the earth
shall be blessed." (Gen. 12:1–3)

God is calling for Abram's complete geographical transplant—
for a move from the only life he has ever known. While the
directions are vague, God's promises are clear and kind.

B. Abram trustingly obeys God. "So Abram went forth as the
Lord had spoken to him" (v. 4a). Although his roots are entrenched in Ur's familiar, highly civilized culture, Abram, age 75,
moves his family to an unknown place.

Listening and Leaving

Put yourself in Abram's position. Why would he leave his
home, a progressive metropolis equivalent to London or
New York, to journey to a new land, following the command
of a god who was not even locally acknowledged? Would
you have gone?

Perhaps God has been speaking to you about your own
roots. Is it time for you to leave familiar territory, to trust
God's faithfulness? If so, it's your move.

III. Faith Expands Understanding (Genesis 13:14–18, 15:1–6)
Abram first heard God's promises of real estate and children before
he left Ur (12:1–3). As Abram obediently leaves his home, God repeats the promises, adding visual confirmation.

"Now lift up your eyes and look from the place where you
are, northward and southward and eastward and west-
ward; for all the land which you see, I will give it to you
and to your descendants forever. And I will make your
descendants as the dust of the earth; so that if anyone
can number the dust of the earth, then your descendants
can also be numbered." (13:14b–16)

Abram was sure that the heir God meant was Eliezer, a house-born
servant (15:2). But God gently sets him straight.

"This man will not be your heir; but one who shall come
forth from your own body, he shall be your heir." (v. 4)

The expansive promise of land was exciting to Abram, but what gave
him the most ecstasy was the renewed promise of a child of his
own. God's promises were being reinforced in ways Abram couldn't

have imagined back in Ur—yet he had followed God before the promises ever seemed attainable. Just like Abram, your understanding of the fullness of God's design will blossom before your very eyes if you, too, will follow Him.

IV. Faith Is No Respecter of Age (Genesis 17:1–8)

Jesus admired the ability of children to simply believe what was told them (Matt. 18:3–4). He loved their spontaneity (Luke 18:16–17). To follow God without hesitancy or duplicity, adults must embrace the same simplicity of faith they had in early childhood. As adults, Abram and Sarai did just that. As they aged, they continued their pursuit of God's will; and as the promises were fulfilled, God changed their names from Abram, meaning "exalted father," to Abraham, "father of a multitude"; and from Sarai, meaning "my princess," to Sarah, "princess" (Gen. 17:5, 15). A ninety-nine-year-old man and an eighty-nine-year-old woman . . . with the faith of little children.

V. Faith Encourages Investment (Genesis 18:1–15)

An investment is an expenditure designed to yield a profitable return. Godly faith is an investment of your life . . . and that investment yields great dividends. Abraham and Sarah invested their lives in following God, and their returns have continued to multiply even to this day (see Gal. 3:8–9)—through the compounded interest of an unlikely dividend, a son.

A. Three visitors (Gen. 18:1–8). Some days hold surprises we could never predict. Abraham's day started calmly enough, but by sundown he was discussing a baby . . . *his* baby! The day reached its zenith when three visitors approached Abraham's tent.

> Now the Lord appeared to him by the oaks of Mamre, while he was sitting at the tent door in the heat of the day. And when he lifted up his eyes and looked, behold, three men were standing opposite him; and when he saw them, he ran from the tent door to meet them, and bowed himself to the earth. (vv. 1–2)

Two of the visitors were angels—one was God.[3] They were unexpected guests, but Abraham's generous arms embraced them. In this act, he would find that hospitality can yield unforeseen rewards.[4]

B. A child promised (18:9–15). While eavesdropping on the conversation between the visitors and her husband, Sarah heard some startling news.

---

3. Genesis 18:13–22 clearly identifies one of the angels as the Lord. This event is known as a theophany, from *theos,* meaning "God," and *phaneros,* meaning "manifest."

4. Rahab's faith also paid dividends to her when she was hospitable to the people of God (James 2:25).

"I will surely return to you at this time next year; and behold, Sarah your wife shall have a son." (v. 10a) How would you react if you were physically unable to have any children and someone suddenly announced you'd soon be giving birth? Would you respond the way Sarah did?

And Sarah laughed to herself, saying, "After I have become old, shall I have pleasure, my lord being old also?" And the Lord said to Abraham, "Why did Sarah laugh, saying, 'Shall I indeed bear a child, when I am so old?' Is anything too difficult for the Lord? At the appointed time I will return to you, at this time next year, and Sarah shall have a son." Sarah denied it however, saying, "I did not laugh"; for she was afraid. And He said, "No, but you did laugh." (vv. 12–15)

We may tend to ridicule Sarah for this seemingly irreverent response; but remember, Abraham also laughed when God approached him about the same promised child (17:15–17).

C. **The child delivered** (21:1–7). Sure enough, Sarah had a son one year later, just as God had promised (vv. 1–2). This woman of ninety and her husband of one hundred named the child Isaac, which is translated "he laughs." Invest your trust in God, and His dividends will astound you.

Investment—Laughing It Off?

Wall Street offers a variety of investment opportunities, but those investments require money. Yet money is not the only resource with which investments and dividends are negotiated (Isa. 55:1–3). Abraham and Sarah invested their lives. They believed God, even when the terms seemed bizarre. And the dividends of their faith came in abundance. Consider the story of Abraham, Sarah, and Isaac—a story of faith. Keep in mind that

without faith it is impossible to please Him, for he who comes to God must believe that He is, and that He is a rewarder of those who seek Him. (Heb. 11:6)

In whom or in what are you placing your trust? And what kind of eternal dividend will that investment yield?

VI. Faith Is Courageous

Sometimes it takes courage to follow God. But faith in God equips the courageous with wisdom and understanding.

" 'Behold, the fear of the Lord, that is wisdom;
And to depart from evil is understanding.' " (Job 28:28)

A. In the face of testing (Gen. 22:1–19, Heb. 11:17–19). Years passed, and Isaac became a young man and the delight of his father. Perhaps Abraham's most difficult test came when God asked him to sacrifice Isaac as a burnt offering (Gen. 22:1–2). Abraham resolutely obeyed, but his heart was convinced that the boy would live (vv. 3, 5; compare Heb. 11:17–19). He truly believed that God would supply a substitute to fulfill the required burnt offering (Gen. 22:8). His courage mounted as he agreed to give up the very possession which God had promised . . . and provided. With knife in hand, Abraham moved deliberately, obediently. And just before the fatal cut, the angel of the Lord intervened and released him from the requirement. Abraham had passed the test (vv. 9–13). As a result, God provided a ram to substitute as a sacrifice—a miraculous conclusion to one man's test of courageous, godly resolve.

B. In the face of a loved one's death (23:1–2). Abraham drank at the deep well of sorrow when Sarah died. Only those who have felt a loss like this can understand bereavement's piercing pang.[5] Even the courageous feel the depth of separation and loneliness when a loved one is taken in death, for godly courage weeps—but not without hope (1 Thess. 4:13). For in hope we know that God causes all things to work together for good— even death (see Rom. 8:28).

C. In the face of one's own death (Gen. 25:1–11). Death eventually visits all. After a satisfying life, Abraham bravely prepared for his own death (vv. 5–8). He was prepared for the inevitable. Would you exhibit this same resolve if you were told today that you had very little time to live? How would you prepare for your own death? If this were the last day of your life, how would you live it?

Wanted: Pioneers of Faith

Have you ever known the exhilaration of exploring uncharted territory? Abraham did. With God's Word as his only map, Abraham blazed a trail of faith for generations to follow.

In hope against hope he believed, in order that he might become a father of many nations, according to that which had been spoken, "So shall your descendants be." And without becoming weak in faith he contemplated his own

---

5. See Cyril J. Barber and Sharalee Aspenleiter's *Through the Valley of Tears* (Old Tappan, N.J.: Fleming H. Revell Co., 1987). This work offers encouragement and guidance for the bereaved.

body, now as good as dead since he was about a hundred years old, and the deadness of Sarah's womb; yet, with respect to the promise of God, he did not waver in unbelief, but grew strong in faith, giving glory to God, and being fully assured that what He had promised, He was able also to perform. (Rom. 4:18–21)

Is God calling you into uncharted territory? A new job maybe? A new set of relationships? A new geographical location? A new opportunity of ministry?

If so, don't be afraid to pack your bags and become a pioneer. The path may be uphill—but the view at the summit is breathtaking!

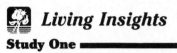 *Living Insights*

Study One

In the life of Abraham we have a rich supply of the human experience. Certainly a model of faith, Abraham was a man of God; yet he was not without flaw. Let's get an overview of his life.

● Read over the story of Abraham's life. Then use the following chart to record any observations you make as you study. Genesis 11 through 25 will serve as your home base for this great biography.

The Life of Abraham	
Verses	Observations

Continued on next page

Verses	Observations

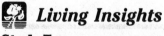 *Living Insights*

Can you identify with some of the experiences or struggles Abraham faced?

- Write down what is going on in your life, describing your spiritual life . . . your family life . . . your financial state. See if any of your circumstances are similar to Abraham's.

An Overview of My Life

_____

_____

_____

_____

_____

_____

_____

_____

_____

_____

Going . . . Not Knowing

Hebrews 11:8–10, Acts 7:2–7

Moving. It has been suggested that as many as forty million Americans do it in any given year.[1] With a few tenaciously clinging exceptions, Americans form a rootless society, a nation of tumbleweeds.

Like the character of Jerry in Edward Albee's *Zoo Story,* many of us could call ourselves "permanent transient[s]."[2] But even though America's demography shifts like a sand dune, not all nomads move for the same reasons. Some move because of a job change or just from general restlessness. Others, however, break away from the secure and move into the unknown because they are prompted by God. That sort of move is always a serendipitous adventure filled with surprise.

I. God Is Full of Surprises

As you turn the pages of biblical history, events emerge that bear record of God's unpredictable leadership. An unexpected universal flood caught the world in its own backwash of rebellion; only Noah and his family were saved, on a vessel they built under God's direction (Gen. 6–7). When fire consumed Sodom and Gomorrah, a few members of Lot's family managed to escape the startling judgment of God (19:23–25). Years later, the Israelites were astonishingly liberated from Egypt after centuries of bondage (Exod. 12:31–33). No less surprising was the fact that they were led by Moses—an eighty-year-old bedouin whose leadership skills had lain dormant for forty years (Exod. 3–4). The fortified walls of Jericho were reduced to rubble during marches choreographed by God through Joshua (Josh. 6). Several centuries later, a palace wall became a blackboard for some mysterious handwriting. The captive Daniel was called to decipher the message, which condemned Belshazzar's kingdom (Dan. 5). And perhaps most surprising of all, a virgin gave birth (Luke 1:26–56, 2:20). Her sinless child settled the sin issue as, through His life and death, God presented His redemptive plan for all humanity (1 Pet. 2:22, 1 John 4:10). Curiously, God often doesn't reveal His plans in full. Rather, He unfolds the map of our journey one section at a time, as Paul's life confirms.

> "And now, behold, bound in spirit, I am on my way to Jerusalem, not knowing what will happen to me there." (Acts 20:22)

---

1. Amitai Etzioni, *An Immodest Agenda: Rebuilding America Before the 21st Century* (New York, N.Y.: McGraw-Hill Book Co., 1983), p. 34.

2. Alvin Toffler, *Future Shock* (New York, N.Y.: Bantam Books, 1971), p. 45.

God's ways often contain an element of surprise. Why doesn't He reveal our entire itinerary? Why does He surprise us with roadblocks and detours and narrow, winding mountain roads? In a nutshell, it's because He wants to teach us that the walk of faith consists of going . . . not knowing.

Shallow Tent Pegs

Tent pegs are designed to secure tents, but it's possible to drive them so deeply into the ground that they become difficult to remove. Just how deep are your tent pegs? Tug at them from time to time. How willing are you to pull them out, pack up the tent, and follow God?

II. When God Surprised Abram

Think about Abram's situation when he was asked to pull up his tent pegs (see Acts 7:2–7).

A. He had strong family ties (Acts 7:2). Ur was Abram's home. It was where he had his livelihood. His family had lived there for generations; Sarai was from Ur as well. These two were deeply rooted in the soil of Mesopotamian culture.

B. He had a clear command from God (7:3). F. B. Meyer graphically depicts God's call:

> Whilst Abraham was living quietly in Ur, protesting against the idolatry of his times, with all its attendant evils, and according to tradition, suffering bitter persecution for conscience sake, "The God of glory appeared unto him, and said, Get thee out of thy country. . . ." When this Divine appearance came we do not know; it may have been in the still and solemn night, or in the evening hour of meditation; or amid the duties of his position: but suddenly there shown from heaven a great light round about him, and a visible form appeared in the heart of the glory, and a voice spake the message of heaven in his ear. Not thus does God now appear to us; and yet it is certain that He still speaks in the silence of the waiting spirit, impressing His will, and saying, "Get thee out." Listen for that voice in the inner shrine of thine heart.[3]

Today God does not normally appear in visions or speak with an audible voice. Instead, He expects us to understand His purposes through Scripture as well as through the desires of our

3. F. B. Meyer, *Abraham; or, The Obedience of Faith* (1968; reprint, Fort Washington, Pa.: Christian Literature Crusade, 1971), p. 13.

own hearts when they are clean before Him (see 2 Tim. 3:16–17, Prov. 3:13–20, Ps. 37:4). The following questions can help you do some personal probing, especially as you consider possible moves. Be sure to examine your answers to understand why you respond the way you do.

1. **Are you uneasy with your current situation?** Are you bored with your present responsibilities? If a worm of gnawing restlessness has eaten into the core of what you used to enjoy, you're probably ready for a change.
2. **Are you searching for new challenges?** Does the prospect of meeting new risks and demands give you an inner surge of curiosity and desire? Such feelings often indicate the anticipation of something more fulfilling.
3. **Are you decreasing your attachment to personal comforts and tangible securities?** Are you winning the battle over the enticement of position, power, and possessions? Do you control your finances, or do they control you? Resolve this issue—your freedom to follow God depends on it.[4]
4. **Are you passionately compelled to obey God?** Walking with Him requires legs of faith. Studying those who walk with God will enhance your knowledge and encourage your spirit (1 Cor. 10:11). But study isn't enough—no one walks with God through someone else's experience. The path is beaten by those who have gone before you. You can follow in their steps, but the shoes you wear must be your own (Heb. 11:6).
5. **Are you tantalized by thoughts of moving to another location?** If so, perhaps God is preparing you for a change of scenery.

> *New Horizons*
>
> If these questions arouse a tingling of anticipation in your spine . . . if the thought of a move is drawing you forward . . . trust God. Let Him take care of the unknowns as He did for Abram, while you concentrate on simply following the Lord—one step at a time.

C. He was given an unsure destination (Acts 7:3). Abram did not know where he was going.

By faith Abraham, when he was called, obeyed by going out to a place which he was to receive for an

---

4. For further study on this idea, see Ron Blue's *Master Your Money* (Nashville, Tenn.: Thomas Nelson Publishers, 1986).

inheritance; and he went out, not knowing where he was going. (Heb. 11:8)

If you told your closest associates you were leaving the area, they would probably ask about your plans. If you began by telling them that God talked to you about going to an unknown distant land, you'd find yourself staring into the faces of some drop-jawed, glassy-eyed folks. There might be some eye-rolling when you told them you did not plan to return, that you planned to take your whole family, and that you planned to camp—without even a fully-equipped recreational vehicle! In Abram's day, the whole plan meant becoming a nomad, and no doubt there were some who thought that would be a crazy move. Countless pilgrims have cancelled their travel arrangements because of the discouraging skepticism of friends and relatives. Abram and Sarai, however, didn't let opinions influence their decision to go.

> **Some Personal Application**
>
> Parents, encourage your children to follow God (Eph. 6:4). And children, don't make it hard for your parents to obey His leading (Col. 3:20).
>
> Following God appears to be risky business. But the real risk lies in the hazards you invite when you ignore His leading. Keep in mind that God understands which paths lead us to the highest good. And we arrive at that pinnacle only through a long series of steps called obedience.

D. He responded obediently (Acts 7:4). To his friends, it must have looked as though Abram had taken leave of his senses. But his mental health was intact. He chose to leave all that was familiar to him because he knew the command came from God, whom he trusted. Had it not been for God's guidance, Abram's actions would have been foolish. Many have trekked out on their own, only to find disappointment, even despair. Abram knew the heart of God; even so, he did not follow God perfectly. God's destination for Abram was Canaan, but Abram initially only made it as far as Haran (Gen. 11:31–32). Contrary to God's counsel, he had allowed his father to join his caravan, and it was probably this influence that cut the journey short.

> **Encourage the Adventurer**
>
> Scripture tells us that Sarai offered Abram no resistance. She never drove her tent pegs so deep that they couldn't be pulled up again.

Nothing is more encouraging than to have the support of others when a life-changing move is planned. Your adventure will be immeasurably enhanced by friends and family who affirm the path God has set before you. Conversely, seek to affirm others as they embark on *their* adventure of faith. That encouragement will help get them over any of the rough roads that might lay ahead.

III. God Is Not Through Surprising His People

It didn't end with Abram; God is calling people to follow Him into new territory even today. In fact, some of you struggle with moving—perhaps at this very moment—and the sweat of uncertainty over God's plan beads your brow. Others of you know what you need to do, and that really causes the perspiration to pour! It's hard to pull up those tenacious tent pegs ... to leave the comforts of home and step out into the unknown. The following questions may help strengthen your pulling power.

A. **Do you seek God's will, or your own?** Are you using your strength to pull up the stakes or to pound them deeper into the ground with the hammer of doubt and apprehension?

B. **Are you as willing to stay as you are to leave?** To say yes may be difficult; it's important to deal with this fundamental issue of availability.

C. **Is your decision to stay or leave becoming more simple or more complicated?** Leaning heavily upon the opinions of people can be a source of confusion after God's way has been made plain in your heart (John 5:44). Once you've made your decision, stand firm—and let God be your security.

Continued on next page

🎴 *Living Insights*

The apostle Peter called believers "aliens and strangers" (1 Pet. 2:11). Certainly Abram would have identified with those words. Let's study them.

• With the help of a concordance, find references to the words *aliens* and *strangers* in the New Testament. Try to gain an understanding of what these words mean for us as Christians today. Jot down your observations in this chart.

Believers . . . Aliens and Strangers	
Verses	Meanings

📖 *Living Insights*

Has the idea of moving been on your mind lately? Perhaps you recently relocated, or maybe you are preparing to. Or maybe you are considering a future move. Our closing applications are worth some further thought. Scribble here any ideas that come to you about your situation.

- Do you seek God's will, or your own?

- Are you as willing to stay as you are to leave?

- Is your decision to stay or leave becoming more simple or more complicated?

Maintaining Vital Contact

Genesis 12:1–9

Paul Tournier, an eminent Swiss physician and psychiatrist, believes each of us needs a personal space—not only in a physical sense but in a social sense as well.

> Man needs a place, and this need is vital to him.... Life is not an abstraction. To exist is to occupy a particular living-space to which one has a right.
>
> Architects and sociologists ought to give thought to this, because man is less conscious of his vital needs, and more ready to disregard them. He allows himself to be herded into compact masses, without realizing that he loses his individuality as a person in a society that is too compact. To exist is to have a place, a space that is recognized and respected by others.[1]

The importance of such a place is also acknowledged in Scripture. Israel's geographical place is the Promised Land.[2] Even when the Israelites' rebellion drove God to herd them into Babylonian captivity, Jeremiah reminded them that God would one day bring them home again.

> " 'And I will be found by you,' declares the Lord, 'and I will restore your fortunes and will gather you from all the nations and from all the places where I have driven you,' declares the Lord, 'and I will bring you back to the *place* from where I sent you into exile.' " (Jer. 29:14, emphasis added)

Israel longed to return to the place of her spiritual heritage. Living in a mobile society tends to minimize our emotional attachment to specific places. But many of us, especially those like the Israelites whose lives are deeply rooted in one location, find a move to an unfamiliar place difficult and fraught with perils.

I. Personal Perils of Leaving the Familiar
Several dangers plague those who are mobile. Let's identify these dangers and learn how we can use them to our advantage, rather than let them dominate us.

    A. The peril of rootlessness. When a plant is separated from the soil, it misses its source of nourishment. Soon it droops and fades, and eventually its leaves fall off. People often reflect that

---

1. Paul Tournier, *A Place For You,* trans. Edwin Hudson (New York, N.Y.: Harper and Row, Publishers, 1968), p. 25.

2. The Abrahamic Covenant includes a place, a nation, and a blessing to Abraham and the entire world (Gen. 12:1–3; 13:14–16; 15:7, 18–21).

same disorientation after a move. Familiar support systems, so important for well-being, are missing. Unless those systems are reestablished, we run the risk of withering, drying up. Old root-ends need to be grafted into new support systems if health is to be restored.

B. The peril of loneliness. Distance separates friends, with the result that friendships become scrapbook memories. We miss the frequent contact and the human exchange of understanding, acceptance, and warmth that were once taken for granted. It takes time to cultivate such relationships—time to grow through the hot and cold seasons of friendship. Moving interrupts that process. A sea of unfamiliar faces and the pain of detachment reminds us that the roots of old friendships need to be nurtured more than ever and that the seeds of new relationships must be watered as well.

C. The peril of insecurity. Unfamiliar territory can intimidate us, incubating insecurity. In a new environment we need to know how to get around, where to shop or go to church, where to find doctors and hospitals. The lack of such supply lines are daily reminders that we've been uprooted from our secure, stable environment.

D. The peril of uncertainty. Inevitably, the unexpected is encountered in a new environment. Neighbors, churches, schools, and stores are not exactly as they were back home. How can we avoid the perils of rootlessness, loneliness, insecurity, and uncertainty? By maintaining daily, vital contact with the Master Gardener, who has moved us to new ground—not to bury us, but to provide fertile soil for our growth.

II. Traveling by Faith: A Biblical Example

Abram's life helps us understand what it means to move with God. Enduring the loss of all that is secure and pressing ahead into unknown territory takes courage. Regular contact with God will foster our courage and hedge us against the perils of moving.

A. Abram was certain of God's leading (Gen. 12:1–4). God spoke very specifically about His plan for Abram:

> Now the Lord said to Abram,
> "Go forth from your country,
> And from your relatives
> And from your father's house,
> To the land which I will show you;
> And I will make you a great nation,
> And I will bless you,
> And make your name great;
> And so you shall be a blessing;

And I will bless those who bless you,
And the one who curses you I will curse.
And in you all the families of the earth shall
   be blessed." (vv. 1–3)

Abram was given a divine deed to foreign real estate, and his children were to become a great nation. He would be blessed and would, in turn, be a blessing to generations of people (see Gen. 14:19, 22:16–18; compare 22:18 with Gal. 3:8–9). In addition, God would honor Abram's children before the nations. God's promise to Abram was unconditional. Abram's response was obedience.

B. Abram was confident in God's strength (Gen. 12:4–5). All Abram's doubts and insecurities had to be put to rest. It was God who had spoken, and it was God who had promised to sustain him.

So Abram went forth as the Lord had spoken to him; and Lot went with him. Now Abram was seventy-five years old when he departed from Haran. And Abram took Sarai his wife and Lot his nephew, and all their possessions which they had accumulated, and the persons which they had acquired in Haran, and they set out for the land of Canaan; thus they came to the land of Canaan.[3] (vv. 4–5)

With every mile Abram traveled, the terrain became less familiar and less appealing. The people he met were different—their language and customs were not like his own. The comfortable sights, sounds, and smells of Haran and Ur had vanished. He was a foreigner. Like Abram, we need God's strength to confront the new customs and values that bombard us in a new place. At those times, the temptation to compromise becomes much harder to resist. God may call us to sail uncharted seas, but we still need a stable rudder, secure riggings, and a stout anchor. Are you facing the trauma of unfamiliar seas? Are your spiritual riggings intact? Are the wind and waves of cultural change blowing you off God's course? Drop your anchor in Hebrews 6:13–19 and claim the promises God gives to those who love and honor Him.

For when God made the promise to Abraham, since He could swear by no one greater, He swore by Himself, saying, "I will surely bless you, and I will surely multiply you." And thus, having patiently waited, he obtained the promise. For men swear by one greater than themselves, and with them an oath given as

3. Haran was a temporary stop on the way from Ur to Canaan (see 11:31, Acts 7:4).

confirmation is an end of every dispute. In the same way God, desiring even more to show to the heirs of the promise the unchangeableness of His purpose, interposed with an oath, in order that by two unchangeable things, in which it is impossible for God to lie, we may have strong encouragement, we who have fled for refuge in laying hold of the hope set before us. This hope we have as an anchor of the soul, a hope both sure and steadfast and one which enters within the veil.

C. **Abram stayed in contact with God** (Gen. 12:6–8). Abram built visual reminders of God's continuing presence in this foreign land.

> And Abram passed through the land as far as the site of Shechem, to the oak of Moreh. Now the Canaanite was then in the land. And the Lord appeared to Abram and said, "To your descendants I will give this land." So he built an altar there to the Lord who had appeared to Him. (vv. 6–7)

Canaanites controlled the land that had been promised to Abram. This was unsettling, to be sure. But God soothed Abram's apprehension with His presence; and Abram, when he arrived at Bethel, constructed an altar where he could continue to call upon God (v. 8). He had established a place of solitude, a place where God could restore his strength and refresh his spirit.

III. **Principles for Maintaining Vital Contact with God**
Temptation to compromise is as close as the nearest newsstand, office party, or business deal. Godliness is tested every day as contrary values vie for our allegiance. As a testimony of his faith and principles, Abram built an altar. You, too, will be better equipped to refuse temptation and compromise if you will draw near to the heart of God. Here are some suggestions to help you erect that altar.

A. **Determine a suitable place to meet.** The best place to get alone with God is one where you will be uninterrupted, comfortable, and free to enjoy God's company.

B. **Commit yourself to a specific time.** Unappropriated time has a way of being swept under the rug of good intentions. Everyone's schedules and needs are different. Tailor a time that fits you best. You may have to rearrange your schedule—cutting here, adding there. But in time you will wonder why you didn't start sooner.

C. **Read great books.** Study the Bible. Read biographies of godly men and women who have been pioneers of faith. Read books that will strengthen your spiritual life.

D. **Write your thoughts in a journal.** Thoughts tend to disentangle themselves as they find expression on paper. Keeping a journal is a great way to record your spiritual pilgrimage, from the mountaintops of hope to the valleys of despair, and all the plateaus of daily life in between.

E. **Secure a truth to share.** Time with God helps you see His perspective. You will find it easier to share God's viewpoint with others when you have spent time with Him alone.

F. **Put a song in your life.** Obtain a hymnal and sing to the Lord (Eph. 5:19). A new dimension of worship will open up to you as your relationship with Him deepens.

Maintaining Vital Contact with God

Where is your special place . . . your altar? If you don't have one, *find* a place to meet with God—a quiet, unhurried place for listening, thinking, enjoying, evaluating, interceding, and worshiping. A place to meet with God. After all, isn't He too good a friend—and too great a God—to neglect?

Living Insights

Study One

Part of maintaining vital contact with the Lord is listening to what He says. God speaks clearly in His Word, the Bible. Let's take a closer look at this rich passage in the book of Genesis.

• One of the most effective methods of personal Bible study is paraphrasing—writing out the biblical text in your own words. Doing this helps extract the meanings and feelings that are beneath the surface of the text. Try this technique on Genesis 12:1–9. Take your time and discover the great treasures in the Word of God.

My Paraphrase of Genesis 12:1–9

_____

_____

_____

_____

_____

_____

_____

_____

_____

_____

_____

_____

_____

_____

_____

_____

_____

_____

_____

_____

 Living Insights

Study Two ▬▬▬▬▬▬▬▬▬▬▬▬▬▬▬▬▬▬▬▬▬▬▬▬

We all need to maintain vital contact with our Lord. In the lesson we discovered six simple steps to establishing a continuing relationship with God. Let's personalize these steps and make them a part of our lives.

• Where will I meet with God?

• What block of time will I commit?

• What will I read?

• When will I start a journal?

• What truths will I share?

• What songbook will I use?

Continued on next page

21

Digging Deeper

A vital walk depends upon daily discernment of the will of God. God could speak audibly with each of us if He desired. However, that is not the norm today. He has left us His Word and His Spirit instead. But some find God's leadership difficult to discern. It needn't be hard or hazardous; but poor judgment has led many far afield. The following guidelines are designed to help you stay on the path of certainty and assurance.

- **Search the Scriptures.** Paul's words to Timothy show four areas of learning that can prove profitable to us (2 Tim. 3:16–17). *Teaching* is profitable because by it we learn about God and His ways. *Reproof* exposes ungodly behavior. *Correction* fixes faulty habits like a splint applied to a broken bone. And *training* teaches us the difference between right and wrong behavior. If you submit yourself to the Word in these four areas, you will be submitting to godly guidance. And you will be adequately equipped to do God's will.

- **Pray for understanding.** God has given every believer a personal strength (see 1 Cor. 12:4–7, 1 Pet. 4:10), and it is His will that we minister according to that ability. God may not be as interested in geography in your case as He was in Abram's. He wants you to develop your gifts no matter where you are. Pray that you may understand what your God-given abilities are.

- **Seek godly counsel.** Godly people incorporate the ways of God into their lives. Their mature judgment is often like spring rain falling on parched ground (Prov. 20:5; 27:17, 19).

- **Be patient.** Take time to make your decisions. Use your doubts to probe other areas of consideration until you come to full rest before God and others (Col. 3:15).

- **Read about God's will.** You will be better prepared to respond to God if you seek to understand how He reveals Himself to His children. Here are several helpful booklets.

Friesen, Garry, and J. Robin Maxson. *Principles for Decision Making: Living According to God's Will.* Portland, Oreg.: Multnomah Press, 1984. The authors stress the use of godly wisdom as a necessary component of knowing God's will.

Swindoll, Charles R. *God's Will: Biblical Direction for Living.* Portland, Oreg.: Multnomah Press, 1981. A booklet for every pilgrim's backpack, this is a concise summary of the methods, concerns, and means by which God reveals Himself.

Yancey, Philip. *Guidance: Making Sense of God's Directions.* Portland, Oreg.: Multnomah Press, 1983. Yancey's booklet explores the cultivation of a sensitive relationship with God as a key element in obtaining His guidance.

When the Godly Slump
Genesis 12:10–20

Aside from notable exceptions, often we expect "holy" men and women to stand apart from the crowd, like superhumans. We put them on pedestals, and we look up to them. But God is not so easily impressed. He knows the stuff from which even leaders are made, and He wants us to remember it too.

We have a tendency to think devoted people do not struggle with the same issues we do. Yet the Scriptures reveal quite the opposite. When people raise their leaders to illegitimate heights, they are rebuked (Acts 10:24–26, 14:11–15). And to further deflate any misconceptions, James, the Lord's brother, clearly indicates that even the prophet Elijah's humanity was no different than the rest of us—"a man with a nature like ours" (James 5:17).[1]

Therefore, godly men and women are simply human, and to say more than this changes the meaning of humanity. For example, take failure—something we all experience. It dogs us like an ever-present shadow on our heels, and with the same vigor it hounds "holy" men and women as well. Just because they are spiritual leaders does not exempt them from the same battles we all face, as we shall see in our lesson for today.

I. A Realistic Fact We Must Never Forget

Introduce a dose of bare-bones reality into your thinking: *Good and godly people fail.* To admire, honor, and respect those whose lives effectively touch others is biblical (1 Thess. 5:12–13). But to deify any man or woman is not. When you exalt someone, you will begin to expect perfection from that person. And that expectation promises only disillusionment. Only God is perfect, and everyone else, whatever their age or position, has a nature that is prone to failure (Rom. 3:23). Often people avoid Christianity because of the failures of so many who profess to be Christians. But it is important to remember that Christians aren't perfect, only forgiven. So don't reject God when human beings disappoint you. God never intended any human to be deified. Grapple with the reality of your own humanity. You fail . . . daily, weekly, continually. All people do—even the godly.

II. Abram Became a Failure Statistic

When tight circumstances pressed Abram, he panicked. Sure, he was "the friend of God" (James 2:23). But he *did* fail. And there are reasons why he did.

---

1. The word *nature* is the Greek *homoiopathēs,* from *homo,* meaning "same," and *pathes,* meaning "to suffer." The words are combined to point to the idea of common suffering. *Homoiopathēs* conveys humanity's common ground . . . the same feelings, circumstances, and experiences shared by all. Acts 14:15 contains the other New Testament usage of *homoiopathēs.*

A. A divine test: a famine. Things are dry in the Promised Land. Days pass without rain. The sun sears the earth, slaking its thirst with the last of the ground's moisture. Plant roots strain for water until, finally, famine grips the land. Food becomes Abram's primary concern. He desperately needs to make a decision—to find some survival plan. His assessment of his circumstances and the course of action he chooses will affect his entire family. He chooses to leave.

> Now there was a famine in the land; so Abram went down to Egypt to sojourn there, for the famine was severe in the land. (Gen. 12:10)

We see no hint of prayer, no turning to God. Just Abram, panicking, watching the harsh environment slowly consume those around him. And he opts to reject God's scorched Promised Land for the greener pastures of Egypt. The severity of the moment tempts Abram to grasp for alternatives; fleeing to Egypt seems the only solution. But that decision brings on a chain reaction of harsh consequences which demand hard choices in the midst of difficult circumstances. You've been there, too, haven't you, at some time in your life?

Acknowledge Life's Difficulties

God invites each of us into the soothing light of His grace. He extends to us help in our trials and comfort in our sorrows. But that does not mean we are instantly freed from the pressures of life. Financial strain and personal struggle may continue long after we commit ourselves to Christ. The curtain does not fall on life's difficult drama when Christ comes on the stage. In fact, pressures may *increase* as a result (John 15:18–27). And in the midst of the problems, hard decisions will have to be made. But think about this:

> Had God pledged Himself to give His servants an unbroken run of prosperity, how many more counterfeit Christians would there be! . . . Do not be surprised if a famine meets you. It is no proof of your Father's anger, but is permitted to come to test you—or to root you deeper, as the whirlwind makes the tree grapple its roots deeper into the soil.[2]

---

2. F. B. Meyer, *Abraham; or, The Obedience of Faith* (1968; reprint, Fort Washington, Pa.: Christian Literature Crusade, 1971), pp. 32–33.

B. A human reaction: off to Egypt. Abram decided to exit the Promised Land to look for relief in Egypt. He had no immediate indication that God was even displeased—God did not stop him; disease did not cripple him. But Egypt was not the real estate God had promised Abram. And disappointingly, we see Abram's convictions colored with compromise.

Consequences of Compromise

The Bible tells of other men of faith who chose compromise. Jonah, instead of going to Nineveh as God commanded, secured passage to faraway Tarshish (Jon. 1:1–3). The legendary strongman, Samson, lingered in the Philistine valley of Sorek and risked his power to a scheming woman (Judg. 16). David's rooftop patio afforded an excellent view of the city . . . and of another man's wife. The door of lust opened and closed almost silently . . . for a while (2 Sam. 11–12). Solomon involved himself with many foreign women. He was a king, the son of David; under his leadership his kingdom's riches increased. Who would suspect that wisdom's greatest proponent was being destroyed from within, apparently unaware of the devastating effects of his compromise (1 Kings 11:1–13)?

Each of these individuals made decisions that eventually brought them personal tragedy. Such decisions are like shackling a ball and chain to your ankle. You may manage OK at first, but soon fatigue sets in; eventually, even walking becomes difficult.

The weighty consequences of compromise are often not immediately noticeable. In time, however, your diminished spiritual vitality will be obvious to all, and the chain's clanking will echo with your every movement.

C. The carnal consequences: Sarai and Pharaoh. Abram's rattling chain of poor judgment is shackled to Sarai's life as well.

> [Abram] said to Sarai his wife, "See now, I know that you are a beautiful woman; and it will come about when the Egyptians see you, that they will say, 'This is his wife'; and they will kill me, but they will let you live. Please say that you are my sister so that it may go well with me because of you, and that I may live on account of you." (Gen. 12:11–13)

Sarai agrees to Abram's request and, by doing so, plays into the snare of deceit.[3]

> The Egyptians saw that the woman was very beautiful. And Pharaoh's officials saw her and praised her to Pharaoh; and the woman was taken into Pharaoh's house. (vv. 14b–15)[4]

Abram realizes a profit from the sacrifice of Sarai's personal integrity. Hear the chain rattle?

> Therefore he [Pharaoh] treated Abram well for her sake; and gave him sheep and oxen and donkeys and male and female servants and female donkeys and camels. (v. 16)

On the surface, Abram prospered. But like so many compromising business and personal decisions, the aftertaste was not as sweet as expected.

> The Lord struck Pharaoh and his house with great plagues because of Sarai, Abram's wife. (v. 17)

Pharaoh was an innocent party; yet, his household became a disaster area. The whole scene doesn't seem fair, does it? Our poor decisions affect more than just ourselves—that ball and chain swings to bruise the ankles of everyone around us.

D. The ultimate outcome: offense and confusion. Pharaoh, though not aligned to Abram's God, knows that he has been given the short end of the stick. And he calls Abram on the royal carpet.

> "What is this you have done to me? Why did you not tell me that she was your wife? Why did you say, 'She is my sister,' so that I took her for my wife? Now then, here is your wife, take her and go." (vv. 18–19)

Applause for Pharaoh; boos and hisses for Abram. Pharaoh was wise enough to deal immediately with the injustice this man of God showed to Sarai and the royal palace. How many non-Christians have been offended by the behavior of Christians? And how many non-Christians have correctly called for accountability in order to stop such shabby behavior? As surely as

---

3. Sarai was not bound to enter into evil just because her husband required it. Husbands and wives are bound to submit to one another (see Eph. 5:21), but the phrase "in the fear of Christ" sets the limits. They are each to adorn themselves with Christlikeness in both their requests and responses. Submission on the part of the husband or wife outside of Christlikeness demeans each person's personal integrity as well as God's original intent (see also Col. 3:18).

4. "As Sarah was then 65 years old ... her beauty at such an age has been made a difficulty by some. But as she lived to the age of 127 ..., she was then middle-aged; and as her vigour and bloom had not been tried by bearing children, she might easily appear very beautiful in the eyes of the Egyptians." C. F. Keil and F. Delitzsch, *Biblical Commentary on the Old Testament* (Grand Rapids, Mich.: William B. Eerdmans Publishing Co., n.d.), vol. 1, p. 197.

Abram's feet etched their toes in the king's carpet, Abram must have been embarrassed by this scene. It would seem that he was now in greater danger of losing his possessions and his life than when he was in the famine. But the king graciously spared him with a biting "Get out!" And Abram and Sarai were on the road again. How much better it would have been if Abram had simply gone to God with his fears and hunger instead of striking out on his own.

A Timeless Lesson

All who subscribe to Christian values are living statements of the truth (2 Cor. 3:2). And we are all governed by this principle: When the godly slump, there are greater ramifications than when others do. No, it doesn't seem fair that the godly should be singled out this way. Christians are, after all, only human. But remember Christ's words, " 'From everyone who has been given much shall much be required' " (Luke 12:48). This admonition clearly states our accountability to God.

The most secure course in any decision is to walk after the Spirit of God (Gal. 5:16–26). By choosing to follow godliness, you will avoid crushing the innocent Sarais of your life, and you'll stay clear of creating problems for the Pharaohs who have come to trust you.

Continued on next page

Living Insights

Abram's decision to go off to Egypt was a choice made without consulting God. Abram didn't pray about this decision . . . he never heard God's voice . . . he didn't think through to the end results. This godly man slumped.

• Another biblical example of a godly man who slumped is the prophet Jonah. Locate his story in your Old Testament and record your observations on the mistakes he made.

Jonah: When the Godly Slump	
Verses	Observations

Living Insights

Even the most godly people are still human and imperfect. Not to acknowledge that would undoubtedly leave you disappointed and disillusioned.

- Have you ever watched one of your heroes fall from the pedestal? What was it like? How did you feel? If you could offer advice to others about this issue, what would you say? Why not use the space below to write a "survival guide" on how to endure the pain of seeing admired leaders fall.

When the Godly Slump: A Survival Guide

_____

_____

_____

_____

_____

_____

_____

_____

_____

_____

_____

_____

_____

_____

_____

_____

_____

A Decision That Led to Disaster

Genesis 13

Adolf Hitler was a man with a driving ambition. He was intoxicated with the vision of a new Rome, and he pursued his dream with uncanny instinct, calculating ruthlessness, and remarkable intellect. His charisma charmed the people of Germany into following him like children to the tune of the Pied Piper's flute. He prophesied that his Third Reich would endure a thousand years.

Twelve years and four months later, the man with the distinctive moustache saw his dream collapse. The architects who designed his vast superstructure of power watched the Allied Forces' demolition crew swing a persistent wrecking ball against its pillars. And with a thunderous crash, the Third Reich fell.

When your mind constructs greedy little empires—with compromised business agreements, illicit relationships, or goals that collide with godliness—destruction is certain. You may be brilliant, gifted, charismatic. But your abilities, used for ungodly pursuits, slice your future into fragments of failure. The Bible invites us to examine the decisions of the people in its pages. Some performed poorly (1 Cor. 10:5–11); others provided examples worth following (Heb. 11:4–40).

I. Decisions Reflect Who You Are

The movies you attend, the friends you select, the decisions you make, even the foods you choose make a statement about you. They reveal your values, your interests, your goals. And with every choice there come consequences . . . some good, some bad. Combine self-lessness with godliness and you have a mixture sweet to the taste. Add selfishness to godlessness and the result is an elixir of disappointment. Abram sipped that awful brew a time or two. Like it or not, his Egyptian experience shows us the state of his heart at the time. His self-centered choices had demoralized his own wife (Gen. 12:13) and perplexed and angered a powerful national leader (vv. 17–20). But the story moves on.

> So Abram went up from Egypt to the Negev, he and his wife and all that belonged to him; and Lot with him. Now Abram was very rich in livestock, in silver and in gold. (13:1–2)

God had promised that Abram would prosper, and prosper he did. Let's read on to see how wealth affected Abram's decisions . . . and how it might impact ours.

A. Wealth tests our decisions (vv. 1–7). Though Abram's cattle multiplied and his gold and silver increased, he soon found that financial stress is not limited to an empty wallet.

Lot, too, became wealthy. Notice Abram's and Lot's different responses to riches. Abram, apparently having learned his lesson, looks beyond his money pouch to his God.

> And he [Abram] went on his journeys from the Negev as far as Bethel, to the place where his tent had been at the beginning, between Bethel and Ai, to the place of the altar, which he had made there formerly; and there Abram called on the name of the Lord. (vv. 3–4)

Lot, on the other hand, shows no such devotion. He "also had flocks and herds and tents" (v. 5). Yet his need for God is not apparent to him. Nevertheless, his holdings—and his uncle's—increase. And so do their problems.

> And the land could not sustain them while dwelling together; for their possessions were so great that they were not able to remain together. (v. 6)

Expanded resources brought Lot's and Abram's herdsmen elbow to elbow. Feuding fractured the two families, and Abram realized something had to be done. As foreigners, a family feud could prove fatal to their freedom, because the native Canaanites and Perizzites could use the occasion to attack and plunder them (v. 7). So the quarrel had to be quelled.

Money Matters

Abram's wealth . . . the widow's mite. Do you accept God's distribution of funds? The haves and the have-nots coexist throughout the pages of Scripture, though not always peacefully! Both are in danger from a deceptively deadly pride.

The have-nots read Scriptures that warn against the pitfalls of prosperity . . . and noses go up in the air. The haves review their bank statements . . . and smugly smile.

In Philippians 4:12, Paul gives us some helpful advice—whether you are the bank president or the night janitor.

> I know how to get along with humble means, and I also know how to live in prosperity; in any and every circumstance I have learned the secret of being filled and going hungry, both of having abundance and suffering need.

So what's the secret to developing this type of perspective? Paul reveals it in verse 11: "I have learned to be content in whatever circumstances I am."

How do you feel about God's distribution of funds? Are you content with your status in life? Or, like Lot, are your eyes constantly scanning the fence lines for greener grass?

B. Consequences follow our decisions (Gen. 13:8–13). Because Abram remembers the lingering effects of his mistakes in Egypt, he makes better choices in his dealings with Lot. No doubt his time of devotion at "the place of the altar" had given him needed perspective for the decisions ahead.

> Then Abram said to Lot, "Please let there be no strife between you and me, nor between my herdsmen and your herdsmen, for we are brothers. Is not the whole land before you? Please separate from me: if to the left, then I will go to the right; or if to the right, then I will go to the left." (vv. 8–9)

Generosity rather than greed ruled Abram's resolution to give his nephew first pick of the property, while Lot cast a calculating eye on the most profitable real estate.

> And Lot lifted up his eyes and saw all the valley of the Jordan, that it was well watered everywhere . . . like the garden of the Lord, like the land of Egypt as you go to Zoar. So Lot chose for himself all the valley of the Jordan; and Lot journeyed eastward. Thus they separated from each other. (vv. 10–11)

Lot crossed decision's narrow bridge with the tall grass of the Jordan Valley enticing him all the way. An Old Testament scholar laments Lot's decision with the somberness of a prophet, "The gradual degeneracy of a relatively good character begins at this point."[1] Another writer amplifies the complexity of Lot's choice.

> Had Lot just held on as he began; had he kept close to Abraham, and had he been content to share Abraham's prospects and prosperity and peace, Lot would have lived a pure and a happy life. . . . What a man chooses, and how a man chooses, when opportunities and alternatives and choices are put before him—nothing more surely discovers a man than that.[2]

Every decision, at least in some way, shapes our destiny. An "uh-oh" echoes forebodingly in our minds as we remember where Lot's lust eventually led him.

> Abram settled in the land of Canaan, while Lot settled in the cities of the valley, and moved his tents as far as Sodom. (v. 12)

Sodom? It's like watching a thunderstorm gathering on the horizon. Could Lot have anticipated the social problems he was buying into? Could Abram have possibly foreseen Lot's future?

1. H. C. Leupold, *Exposition of Genesis* (Grand Rapids, Mich.: Baker Book House, 1965), vol. 1, p. 436.

2. Alexander Whyte, *Bible Characters* (London, England: Oliphants, 1959), vol. 1, pp. 81–82, 84.

Now the men of Sodom were wicked exceedingly and
sinners against the Lord. (v. 13)

Lot's "greener grass" is luring him toward disaster.

C. **Values are reflected in our decisions** (vv. 14–18). Graciousness became gain for Abram. After Lot's departure, God appeared to Abram and told him that all the land he could see in any direction would belong to him and his descendants (vv. 14–15). Abram's response reveals that he understood where the true riches lie.

Then Abram moved his tent and came and dwelt by
the oaks of Mamre, which are in Hebron, and there
he built an altar to the Lord. (v. 18)

While Lot moved into tall grass, Abram shifted his operation to the hills of Hebron where he worshiped the Lord.

II. Making Decisions Today

Abram and Lot made decisions that paved the paths of their futures—in opposite directions. Let's draw some principles of decision making from their experiences.

A. **Always look beyond the benefits promised by opportunity.** Children see and suddenly want, unable to look beyond the immediate. Likewise, immature adults fail to consider the long-range results of their decisions. For example, we behave like children when we use charge cards without considering the long-term cost. Not every opportunity to satisfy our desires is a good one. We must learn to weigh the cost of our decisions— not only for the present but for the future as well.

B. **Never underestimate the impact of bad decisions.** If you choose immediate gratification, the impact of your choice is likely to come in a delayed and devastating explosion. How could Lot have possibly anticipated the danger to his family when his intent was the well-being of his herds? How can we focus only upon making a living? Learn to list and closely examine both the promises and the pitfalls of opportunities.

C. **Forget about pleasing only yourself.** Self-centeredness is the twin of instant gratification. If you choose only for yourself, others will suffer and relationships will fail. Study Jesus' unselfish ministry (Mark 10:45) and God's unswerving focus on the needs of others (Matt. 9:36–38, Phil. 2:3–5).

D. **Greater freedom of choice demands stronger discipline and accountability.** Abram allowed Lot to freely choose the land he wanted, subduing his own natural desires. He knew he was accountable to God and perhaps remembered that previous decisions to gratify himself had proven disastrous. How about you? Are you learning from your mistakes? Let their echo remind you to refine your priorities and renew your accountability to God.

 Living Insights

Study One ━━━━━━━━━━━━━━━━━━━━━━━━━━━━━━━

The story found in Genesis 13 has many lessons to teach us. Let's take a closer look at them.

- Read Genesis 13. List a dozen key words and write definitions for them. You may want to consult a Bible dictionary. Next, jot down the significance of each word, asking yourself the question, Why is this word important to the text?

Genesis 13

Key word: _____

Definition: _____

Significance: _____

Key word: _____

Definition: _____

Significance: _____

Key word: _____

Definition: _____

Significance: _____

Key word: _____

Definition: _____

Significance: _____

Key word: _____

Definition: _____

Significance: _____

Key word: _____

Definition: _____

Significance: _____

Key word: _____

Definition: _____

Significance: _____

Key word: _____

Definition: _____

Significance: _____

Key word: _____

Definition: _____

Significance: _____

Key word: _____

Definition: _____

Significance: _____

Key word: _____

Definition: _____

Significance: _____

Key word: _____

Definition: _____

Significance: _____

Living Insights

Study Two

No one is immune from the effects of bad decisions. Are you comfortable with your methods of reaching good decisions?

- Write down the steps you take to make important decisions. Ask the Lord to show you if there are things about this process that you need to change.

Continued on next page

How I Make Decisions

_____

_____

_____

_____

_____

_____

_____

_____

_____

_____

_____

_____

_____

_____

_____

_____

_____

_____

_____

_____

_____

Abraham, the Greathearted

Genesis 14

1189 A.D.: Round 3 of the Christians versus the Muslim Turks. The stakes? Access to the Holy Land and the rescue of Syrian Christians. Three kings joined ranks against the forces of the Muslim leader, Saladin; one was German, one was French, and one was English.

As it turned out, the German drowned and the Frenchman fled, leaving Richard I to face the intimidating Saladin, alone.

The crusade was costly. But the valor of its winner earned him a name that has stuck through the centuries—Richard the Lionhearted.

If Richard I could be called the Lionhearted, certainly Abram qualifies for the name Greathearted. Two men in history . . . one of unusual bravery, the other of unusual greatness.

I. Characteristics of Greatness

The Bible gives clear qualifications for personal greatheartedness.

A. Genuine unselfishness. Greed and possessiveness are often the snares that trip up our efforts to be unselfish. Generosity, on the other hand, frees us from those traps and is the hallmark of a greathearted person.

> Do nothing from selfishness or empty conceit, but with humility of mind let each of you regard one another as more important than himself; do not merely look out for your own personal interests, but also for the interests of others. (Phil. 2:3–4)

B. Willingness to sacrifice. People are of supreme importance to God. Giving to others at your own expense is an act which models greatheartedness in His eyes. Remember the example of Paul:

> For you recall, brethren, our labor and hardship, how working night and day so as not to be a burden to any of you, we proclaimed to you the gospel of God. (1 Thess. 2:9)

C. Pure motives. God examines not only our deeds but our motives as well. Greatheartedness is never inspired by the hope of personal gain or recognition. Jesus' commendation of Nathanael, an Israelite "in whom is no guile," shows him to be a model for us to follow (John 1:47). Treachery, deceit, greed, and wickedly devised schemes were not his allies. He had no hidden agenda or manipulative motives.

D. Restraint of power. Wisdom and greatness attend the person who uses authority as God intended.

It is an abomination for kings to commit wickedness, for a throne is established on righteousness. (Prov. 16:12)

It's easy to see power as an opportunity to control others, but greathearted people resist that temptation.

Go for Greatness

Greatness has many standards: how much you own, where your office is located, how well you are socially connected.

God is not so easily impressed by such status symbols. Yet, He does recognize your need for recognition. In fact, greatness is a legitimate personal goal. Jesus Himself clarified this issue for His disciples when they struggled over the same issue.

"You know that the rulers of the Gentiles lord it over them, and their great men exercise authority over them. It is not so among you, but whoever wishes to become great among you shall be your servant, and whoever wishes to be first among you shall be your slave; just as the Son of Man did not come to be served, but to serve, and to give His life a ransom for many." (Matt. 20:25–28)

If greatness is your goal, then seek it God's way. Instead of bossing people around, serve them—sincerely ... selflessly ... sacrificially. ●

II. Abram, the Greathearted

Abram's unselfishness, self-sacrifice, pure motives, and righteous use of authority set him apart as a great man. Let's take a closer look at his life to see how these traits show up.

A. Abram's release of the Jordan Valley to Lot reveals unselfishness. Abram, as the eldest and the leader of the family, had the right to claim the choicest land, yet he relinquished that prerogative to his nephew. As you'll recall, however, Lot's choice brought unanticipated consequences (compare Gen. 13:12–13 with 18:20–19:29).

B. Abram's rescue of Lot displays love at personal cost. When Lot was choosing land, his eyes were too full of lush green grass to see the problems poisoning the soil. The valley had been controlled by Mesopotamian kings for twelve years, and Lot and his family arrived just in time for the rebellion. They, along with the other defeated valley inhabitants, were taken into captivity (14:11–12). When Abram receives the news, he mobilizes his allies, the Amorites, and comes to the rescue.

1. **His response is immediate** (v. 14a). Abram doesn't wait until he has time. He doesn't gloat over the results of Lot's selfishness. He drops what he is doing and goes.

2. **His response is costly** (v. 14b). Abram leaves his herds and his family. He risks his own life and the lives of his friends. He runs the chance of being captured himself. Why? Because a wayward nephew needs his help. He models the attitude a New Testament writer later put into words:

> But whoever has the world's goods, and beholds his brother in need and closes his heart against him, how does the love of God abide in him? Little children, let us not love with word or with tongue, but in deed and truth. (1 John 3:17–18)

3. **His response is effective** (Gen. 14:15–16). The Mesopotamians don't know Abram exists. The advantage of surprise and the wise use of darkness give Abram the advantage at Dan, the intercept point 130 miles north of the oaks of Mamre. Abram divides and conquers, as ancient strategists have done before him, and defeats an army that had gone undefeated for more than a decade.

C. His motives are pure (vv. 17–24a). Abram's intent was to save his nephew; in so doing, he saved a nation as well. And overnight, he became a hero (v. 17)! But in the hubbub of sudden popularity, he remains humble—even when prestigious people knock on his door.

1. **Abram's response to a righteous king** (vv. 18–20). Melchizedek is a friendly king from the "city of peace"—the future Jerusalem.[1] When he hears of Abram's victory, he comes to congratulate him, bringing food and wine to the tired troops and blessings to their leader. Most people's heads would swell at an honor like that. But Abram, realizing Melchizedek is a priest as well as a king, responds by graciously tithing a tenth of the war spoil.

2. **Abram's response to an unrighteous king** (vv. 21–24). Sodom's king, Bera, pays a visit to Abram also—though not to bless him. Since Abram is the conqueror, Bera has no legal claim to the spoil. Without so much as a muttered

---

1. Both *El* and *Elyon* are used by Melchizedek as Canaanite designations for Yahweh. How did Melchizedek come to know Abram's God? For a provocative study of Melchizedek's commitment to the "God Most High" *(El Elyon)*, see Don Richardson's *Eternity in Their Hearts* (Ventura, Calif.: GL Publications, Regal Books, 1981), pp. 5–11.

"Thanks" to Abram for saving his people, he delivers his resentful message:

"Give the people to me and take the goods for yourself." (v. 21)

Abram's response proves his untainted motives:

"I have sworn to the Lord God Most High, possessor of heaven and earth, that I will not take a thread or a sandal thong or anything that is yours, lest you should say, 'I have made Abram rich.' " (vv. 22–23)

D. He doesn't misuse authority. It's obvious in Abram's encounter with Bera that the two of them operate with different values. Abram had earned power by freeing Bera's people. Yet rather than forcing his leadership upon them, he returns them to their king and goes home . . . with no more men than he had brought.

"I will take nothing except what the young men have eaten, and the share of the men who went with me, Aner, Eshcol, and Mamre; let them take their share." (v. 24)

The Hero of Our Hearts

Richard the Lionhearted demonstrated courageousness on the field of battle. Abram, centuries earlier, demonstrated greatheartedness, not only on the field of battle, but in the context of family life. He gave rather than hoarded. He responded to need when help was required. He kept his heart pure. And he used authority to benefit others. All of his achievements reflect a greathearted man.

Richard I may be the hero of our battlefields, but Abram should be the hero of our hearts. For it is within the heart that the greatest battles are fought.

Living Insights

In this study we learned four characteristics of greatheartedness seen in Abram's life. Can you think of other biblical characters who have demonstrated these same traits?

Genuine Unselfishness

_____   _____

_____   _____

_____   _____

_____   _____

Willingness to Sacrifice for Others

_____   _____

_____   _____

_____   _____

_____   _____

Pure Motives

_____   _____

_____   _____

_____   _____

_____   _____

Restraint of Power

_____   _____

_____   _____

_____   _____

_____   _____

Continued on next page

![icon] *Living Insights*

Could the term *greathearted* be used to describe you? Rate yourself in the four characteristics of greatness we studied in this lesson, with 5 being best and 1 being worst. Then jot down a plan for improving your weaker areas.

Genuine Unselfishness   1   2   3   4   5

_____

_____

_____

Willingness to Sacrifice for Others   1   2   3   4   5

_____

_____

_____

Pure Motives   1   2   3   4   5

_____

_____

_____

Restraint of Power   1   2   3   4   5

_____

_____

_____

A Vision, a Dialogue, a Covenant
Genesis 15

Henry Luce, founder of Time-Life, Inc., amassed a financial empire while revolutionizing modern journalism. He frequently reflected upon his boyhood years in Shantung, China, where his father served as a missionary. Alan Loy McGinnis retells one memory:

> In the evenings he and his father had gone for long walks outside the compound, and his father had talked to him as if he were an adult. The problems of administering a school and the philosophical questions occupying him were all grist for their conversational mill. "He treated me as if I were his equal," said Luce. Their bond was tight because they were friends, and both father and son were nourished by the relationship.[1]

The warmth between this father and son is mirrored in the stories of Abram and his God. Abram was called "the friend of God" (James 2:23). The phrase implies that the two of them knew each other well, spent time together, were comfortable in one another's presence. It also suggests that they were committed to each other and took delight in their relationship . . . like all good friends should.

I. A Personal Conversation (Genesis 15:1–8)
The fifteenth chapter of Genesis lets us peer in the window of Abram's friendship with God. Much has happened in Abram's life since God made His promises—a long caravan to Canaan, a panicky escape to Egypt, mistakes with Sarai, his war with international forces. In the wake of these events, we find Abram in need of reassurance. Let's look in and eavesdrop on the conversation.

A. A vision (v. 1). We all know people who have vision, or goals for the future (Prov. 29:18). But Abram's vision is of a different kind—a visit from God. The vision extends through the entire chapter without a break and serves to abate Abram's insecurity about his circumstances.

B. A dialogue (Gen. 15:2–8). Dialogue is two-way conversation; now, Abram speaks and God responds.

1. **Abram speaks** (vv. 2–3). Basically, he is inquiring, "What is Your plan? How can You give me descendants, since I have no son and my slave Eliezer stands to be my only heir?" Jumping to false conclusions is easy when waiting stretches from weeks to months to years, as it did in Abram's case. Weary with waiting, we sometimes feel that God's plans

---

1. Alan Loy McGinnis, *The Friendship Factor* (Minneapolis, Minn.: Augsburg Publishing House, 1979), p. 10.

need a little help to get them going. But then we learn, like Abram, that God's way of doing things is often contrary to what we feel is natural and expected.

2. **God responds** (vv. 4–5). The Lord's reply is strong, revealing that Abram's logic has brought him to the wrong conclusion and that God's plan actually centers on a child to be sired by Abram himself. The Lord further unfolds the plan as He speaks of Abram's future: " 'Now look toward the heavens, and count the stars.... So shall your descendants be' " (v. 5).

3. **Abram believes.** Abram must have gazed at the night sky in awe as confidence in God's plan settled again into his heart.

> Then he believed in the Lord; and He reckoned
> it to him as righteousness. (v. 6)

God's Reckoning

Abram received God's reckoning when he believed. *Reckon* is a word with financial connotations, meaning "credit to an account." And in the business world, when debits are balanced by credits, the account is "paid up." Similarly, when God received Abram's trust as credit, He responded by releasing him from any debit of sin. Abram's faith caused God to write on Abram's sin ledger "Paid in Full."

What is the status of your sin ledger? Has God stamped on it, "Paid in Full"? Jesus Himself declares the opportunity you have to clear your debt with God: " 'Whoever believes in Him should not perish, but have eternal life' " (John 3:16b). And *whoever* responds, like Abram, can be assured that their sin ledger has been paid up. When you come to Him in faith, He will freely give you forgiveness in return,

> having canceled out the certificate of debt
> consisting of decrees against us and which
> was hostile to us; and He has taken it out
> of the way, having nailed it to the cross.
> (Col. 2:14)[2]

If your sin account has not yet been stamped "Paid in Full," won't you come to Him with all your debts and lay them at the foot of the cross?

---

2. For further study on the relationship of faith to works, see Zane C. Hodges's *The Gospel Under Seige* (Dallas, Tex.: Redención Viva, 1981).

4. God affirms (Gen. 15:7). God reminds Abram of His promise of land (see vv. 18–21). Nothing new to Abram . . . God has periodically and patiently reinforced that promise (12:1b, 13:14–17). But Abram needs to hear it again because he, like us, is engaged in busy, day-to-day activities that drown out the voice of God.

5. Abram questions (15:8). Reassurance and affirmation are often twin needs in our walk with God. At times we could easily echo Abram's request—God, how can I know You'll do as You said? To such a question we would expect a rebuke from God for Abram's lack of faith. But what we find instead is a revelation.

II. A Prophetic Revelation (Genesis 15:9–21)

God reveals a glimpse of His plan to His uncertain friend.

A. Birds and animals formalize the prophecy (vv. 9–11). God instructs Abram to bring a heifer, a female goat, a ram, a turtledove, and a pigeon. Abram does and then cuts each of the animals in two.

> The animals chosen . . . corresponded exactly to the ritual of sacrifice. Yet the transaction itself was not a real sacrifice, since there was neither sprinkling of blood nor offering upon an altar . . . and no mention is made of the pieces being burned. The proceeding corresponded rather to the custom, prevalent in many ancient nations, of slaughtering animals when concluding a covenant, and after dividing them into pieces, of laying the pieces opposite to one another, that the persons making the covenant might pass between them.[3]

God uses this familiar Chaldean covenant to convince Abram that He would make good on His promise. Abram understands the legal implications of the Lord's actions. But the covenant has a symbolic meaning as well—God's children would face dark days.

B. Darkness intensifies the prophecy (vv. 12–17). As the sun dips behind the horizon, night falls, and a deep sleep comes over Abram. A great darkness descends upon him, and terror floods his mind like a nightmare. But what Abram actually sees and hears are events of the future involving God's covenanted children.

---

3. C. F. Keil and F. Delitzsch, *Biblical Commentary on the Old Testament* (Grand Rapids, Mich.: William B. Eerdmans Publishing Co., n.d.), vol. 1, pp. 213–14.

1. **Abram's children would be aliens and slaves** (v. 13). God reveals a slice of the future—the Hebrews were to fall into the hands of the Egyptiåns. They would suffer for more than four hundred years before being delivered from their captors (v. 16, Exod. 12:40).[4]
2. **Abram would live to a good old age** (Gen. 15:15). We find the meaning of a "good old age" in chapter 25, verses 7 and 8. This prophecy introduces a brighter theme and serves to impress Abram with the accuracy and vastness of God's knowledge, not only of the promised son and his offspring, but also of his own personal life.
3. **Abram's children would be an instrument of divine judgment** (15:16b). During Israel's years under Egypt's harsh yoke, the nations occupying the Promised Land would be spiraling deeper into moral decadence. Israel's final deliverance from bondage would facilitate God's judgment upon these other nations. In this prophecy, God allows Abram to see that He does not deal with His people in isolation. Rather, domestic and foreign events are interwoven to accomplish broader objectives—objectives which Abram was totally unaware of at the time. God's plans thread together like a tapestry for a purposeful design.
4. **God would rescue Abram's descendants** (vv. 17–18a). A smoking oven and a fiery torch passed through the halved animals, which confirmed the covenant and foreshadowed the manner in which the escaping Hebrews would be led in the wilderness—with a cloud by day and a fiery column by night (Exod. 13:21–22).
5. **Abram's children would be restored to the Promised Land** (Gen. 15:18b–21). Although the Israelites eventually lived in Canaan, to this day they have never extended themselves to the borders God established. Aspects of God's covenant with Abram are still lingering, waiting to be fulfilled one day before a watching world.

III. Some Personal Perspectives

Abram's personal need for understanding is one we all share. Here are several perspectives to help clarify God's purposes for our lives.

A. God understands our fears and listens to our questions. Abram isn't rebuked or chided for raising questions about God's purposes. Instead, the Lord graphically responds

---

4. For a complete discussion on the length of the Hebrews' stay in Egypt and the date of the Exodus, see Gleason L. Archer's *A Survey of Old Testament Introduction* (Chicago, Ill.: Moody Press, 1964), pp. 211–23.

to each concern. Our Father also patiently gives us reassurance during our own dark days, when the promises seem uncertain and circumstances seem confusing. God hears not only the exclamation marks of faith, but the question marks of doubt. And He not only hears, He cares (Luke 18:1–8, 1 Pet. 5:6–7).

B. Dark times do not overshadow hope. The future seemed uncertain to Abram until God showed him the role his family would play. Isn't it precisely when we understand how we fit into God's plan that we become encouraged (Jer. 29:11)?

C. A delay must not be considered a cancellation. God's schedules do not always coincide with ours. When God says to wait, it is because He knows how the events of our lives fit together. Satan would have us interpret the "wait" as God ignoring us for more important matters. Enduring the "wait" has its own built-in purposes and rewards, not only for us, but for others as well (Ps. 40:1–3, Heb. 10:35–36).

D. Our future is clearer to God than our past is to us (Ps. 139:1–6). He knew Abram's life span. He knows ours as well. We can surely trust the One who knows every detail of our past, present, and future infinitely better than we ever could.

A Friend for All Seasons

Abram was God's friend—a mind-boggling thought when you consider it.

It may seem inconceivable that the same God wants such a relationship with you. You are a creature he made. You are a sinner he redeemed. You are even his child by adoption and by supernatural new birth. Yet he calls you to a higher dignity—to that of friend and partner. "No longer do I call you servants," Jesus told his disciples, "for the servant does not know what his master is doing; but I have called you friends, for all that I have heard from my Father I have made known to you" (John 15:15). He *chose* you to be such.

Two facts necessarily follow. If you are his friend, he will share his thoughts and plans with you. If you are his partner, he will be concerned about your views on his plans and projects. Whatever else prayer may be, it is intended to be a sharing and a taking counsel with God on matters of importance to him. God has called

47

you to attend a celestial board meeting to deliberate with him on matters of destiny.[5]
Think about that for a minute. If that doesn't turn you
on—you don't have any switches!

Living Insights

Study One

"Without faith it is impossible to please Him" (Heb. 11:6). Let's take
a closer look at what faith is all about.

- Hebrews 11 is often referred to as faith's Hall of Fame. Read through
  this great chapter and list the key characters. How did their faith
  help them in life? Record your answers below.

Hebrews 11

Character: _____ Verse: _____

How faith helped: _____

_____

Character: _____ Verse: _____

How faith helped: _____

_____

Character: _____ Verse: _____

How faith helped: _____

_____

Character: _____ Verse: _____

How faith helped: _____

_____

Character: _____ Verse: _____

How faith helped: _____

_____

5. John White, *Daring to Draw Near: People in Prayer* (Downers Grove, Ill.: Inter-Varsity Press,
1977), p. 17.

Character: _____ Verse: _____

How faith helped: _____

_____

Character: _____ Verse: _____

How faith helped: _____

_____

Character: _____ Verse: _____

How faith helped: _____

_____

Character: _____ Verse: _____

How faith helped: _____

_____

Character: _____ Verse: _____

How faith helped: _____

_____

Living Insights

Study Two ━━━━━━━━━━━━━━━━━━━━━━━━━━━━━━━━━

After learning about people like those we listed in Study One, it's quite natural to want to possess the faith of such great men and women. The beauty of this subject is that faith of this magnitude *is* available to regular, everyday people like us.

• Are you a person of faith? Let's spend our Living Insights time praying about this issue. Ask God to help you see how you can grow in faith in the days ahead. Talk to God about your fears for tomorrow. Make this occasion a rich time of unguarded conversation between you and your Father.

When You Run Ahead, *Watch Out!*

Genesis 16

Dilemmas. We all face them ... like when two good TV shows air at the same time ... or when the Bible study you're interested in meets on your bowling night.

Sometimes the conflict is more serious. Occupational dilemmas occur when the best-paying job is not the job you would enjoy. You may face an academic crossroad when the graduate degree that would further your career encroaches on precious time with your family. Or how about the constant rub between living on a fixed income and wanting to splurge on special occasions that aren't in the budget? And there's the daily tug-of-war between fatigue and your attempt to keep physically fit.

But perhaps the most frustrating dilemma of all is the yearning to make things happen *now,* when God seems to be saying *wait.*

I. Dilemmas Today

Impatience needles us to act before it is time. Have you faced dilemmas like these?

A. The lost friend dilemma. You have an unsaved friend with whom you have discussed the claims of Christ. She has asked you to back off, but you've recently discovered that she has a terminal illness. You pray, but it seems God hasn't opened the door of opportunity to approach her again. Do you stay quiet, or speak up?

B. The romance dilemma. You have fallen in love with Mr. Right. *You* believe he is the one for you, but he doesn't have a clue that you're even interested. Do you drop hints, or do you just wait and see how the relationship develops, hoping he will eventually get the message?

C. The debt dilemma. You are confident that God is leading you into Christian ministry, but you are deeply in debt. Do you ignore your financial obligations and begin your training anyway? Or do you take the time to pay back what you owe plus save enough to cover your expenses?

II. Dilemmas from History

Several Bible characters found themselves swept into a sea of painful consequences by the undertow of their own impatience.

A. Moses' dilemma (Exod. 2, Acts 7). Moses knew God had appointed him to deliver His people from Egyptian bondage (Acts 7:25). But rather than wait upon God to accomplish the task His way, Moses took matters into his own hands, angrily killing an Egyptian who was beating a Hebrew slave (Exod. 2:11–12).

Instead of the people applauding Moses for his forceful leadership, they questioned his authority (Acts 7:27–28). Consequently, he fled Egypt to protect his life and remained in exile for forty years (vv. 29–30). It would be interesting to know how differently biblical history would have been written had Moses waited for God's solution to his dilemma.

B. Saul's dilemma (1 Sam. 13). Saul, caught in a potentially hopeless situation, waited for the prophet-priest Samuel to meet him in Gilgal and offer a burnt offering to God—a job only a priest could lawfully perform. Saul gathered his men and waited . . . and waited. The agreed seven days Samuel told Saul to wait passed, but there was no sign of Samuel (v. 8). Thinking Saul was a fool to delay the sacrifice, his men began to defect. Should the king wait for Samuel—just sit by and watch his standing army deteriorate? Or should he officiate the sacrifices himself in order to restore the people's confidence in him? Saul succumbed to panic; he decided to officiate the sacrifice himself rather than wait for Samuel (vv. 9–10). Consequently, he lost his throne (vv. 11–14).

C. Abram's dilemma (Gen. 16). God had ratified His promise and reminded Abram that he would father a child. However, instead of waiting, Abram and Sarai began to rationalize their situation, and their impatience produced a foolish plan. At Sarai's request, Abram took Sarai's handmaiden Hagar and fathered a child through her (v. 4). That child would become the father of the Arab nations (21:18). Later, Sarai would have her own promised child, and that son would be the heir of Abram's blessing (v. 2). Generations to come would feel the permanent pain of the decision Abram and Sarai made in haste.[1]

Making Wise Decisions

Dilemmas heighten our need to make the right choices. Therefore, looking to Scripture for help in the decision-making process is a wise step. Psalm 119 acknowledges several principles that can positively direct our decisions.

- Seek the Lord with all your heart (v. 2). This pursuit will produce such a transformation in you that your thinking will increasingly represent God's perspective.

---

1. The modern Arab/Israeli conflict began here, as the sons of Ishmael and the sons of Isaac comprise these two nations, respectively. Wilbur Smith's *Israeli/Arab Conflict . . . and the Bible* (Ventura, Calif.: G/L Publications, Regal Books, 1967) effectively addresses the subject.

- Acknowledge the Word of God as a lamp (v. 105). God's truth sheds light on life's most darkened paths so that you may walk securely.
- Cultivate responsiveness to God's counsel (v. 129). As you become more sensitive to God, you will gain further understanding of life, therefore making sense out of your dilemmas and making decisions much clearer and easier.
- Pursue wisdom (vv. 98–100). Your ability to apply wisdom to your decisions will mark you as a wise person (see also Prov. 2, James 1:5).

Perhaps you are in the midst of a dilemma, or see one approaching. Faithfully follow these steps, and you will learn to accurately assess your dilemmas and make the wisest decisions for eternity.

III. A Close-up of Abram's Dilemma

Let's put Abram's dilemma under a microscope and focus in on the details.

A. Schemes from within: tampering with the promise (Gen. 16:1–4a). God promised Abram a child, but He did not specifically say Sarai would be the mother. You can see the wheels turning in Sarai's mind. "I'm old and barren. Hagar, my handmaiden, is young and able. A surrogate mother! Abram, I have an idea. . . . " It's a logical solution. Haven't they waited ten years, since arriving in Canaan, for the child? Abram is in his mid-eighties and not getting any younger. Surely, thinks Sarai, something has to be done immediately, so she encourages Abram to impregnate her more fertile handmaiden. At this time, no social stigma was attached to what Abram did, as custom allowed a barren wife to call on a substitute to bear a child on her behalf.[2] But God's ways often conflict with socially practiced norms. Once again, there is no record of Abram or Sarai seeking the Lord in a moment of crisis. In fact, their rationalization upstages their loyalty to God and even to one another. In essence, they agree to a plan which amounts to using adultery to accomplish God's purpose.

B. Pressures from without: dealing with the consequences (vv. 4b–7). Basic physics teaches that for every action there is an opposite and equal reaction. Human relationships are subject to the same laws. As conflict erupts in Abram's household, a chain reaction is set in motion.

2. John Bright, *The History of Israel* (Philadelphia, Pa.: The Westminster Press, 1959), p. 71.

1. **Hagar despises Sarai** (v. 4b). Hagar's pregnancy changes the way she views her employers. Suddenly, her own position as the mother of Abram's child seems more important than Sarai's position as Abram's wife; so, consequently, Hagar looks down her nose at the barren woman.

2. **Sarai blames Abram** (v. 5). Though Sarai had initially given Abram the green light, she is now flashing raging red. "How could you?" she demands. "I thought that's what you wanted," Abram responds in confusion. Abram is between the proverbial rock and a hard place. Pressure mounts, and he blurts out another poor decision: " 'Behold, your maid is in your power; do to her what is good in your sight' " (v. 6a).[3]

3. **Hagar becomes a victim** (v. 6b). Sarai's harsh jealousy drives away Hagar—the maidservant whose only role in this affair was obedience to her masters. And Abram, whose goal is peace at any price, declines to interfere. He could have arranged to care for this woman and his child. But Abram buckles under household tensions, and Hagar's dignity is disregarded.

C. **Mercy from above: consoling the broken** (vv. 7–14). An unwed mother needs compassion, not condemnation. The angel of the Lord visits Hagar, as she hides near a spring, to offer His comfort and help.[4]

1. **God gives Hagar a chance to explain** (v. 8). God wants to hear Hagar's side of the story; and she answers honestly, hiding nothing.

2. **God advises Hagar to return home** (v. 9). God's solution to Hagar's dilemma requires her to submit to Sarai—a big change in attitude—for Hagar needs the protection provided there.

3. **God reveals Hagar's future** (vv. 10–14). Instead of wasting away in the wilderness, she will be the mother of many descendants (v. 10). Her child will be a boy named Ishmael, which means "God hears" (v. 11). His character will be untameable like a wild stallion, beautiful but unbridled, spreading antagonism everywhere he roams (v. 12).

---

3. Custom further dictated that if a son were born to a surrogate mother, neither the mother nor the son could be forced to leave. Abram not only overlooked the needs of Hagar as a person who had given herself to the whims of her masters, but he also disregarded the age-old custom of the land. See John Bright, *The History of Israel*, p. 71.

4. The *angel of the Lord* (v. 7) is a self-manifestation of God (Gen. 31:11, 13; Judg. 5:23, 6:11–24, 13:3–22). Since the angel of the Lord does not appear in the New Testament, He is believed to be the preincarnate Christ (John 1:1–2, 14).

4. **Hagar responds with hope** (vv. 13–14). She expresses humble delight at God's presence. His love has touched her needs. She marks this significant occasion by naming the spring Beerlahairoi, meaning "the well of the living One who sees me."

D. Realities to face: decisions bear fruit (vv. 15–16, Gal. 6:7–8). Ishmael is born, and Abram and Sarai are still fourteen years away from the promised child. They will have to live with Ishmael, watching him pass through childhood into his teens before God will give them their own child. Every day they taste the bitter fruit of their improvident decision and are reminded of their failure to wait upon God.

IV. Defusing Dilemmas

The next time you are tempted to sprint ahead of God's best for you, run your dilemma through these simple checks.

A. Walk a little slower. If the decisions facing you are creating a pressure cooker inside your head, slow down. Take a long walk, sort out the issues confronting you, and reflect on the promises of God. There is an appointed time for everything (Eccles. 3:1). Is it time to wait, or time to advance?

B. Ask God for patience. A slower pace, together with wisdom and self-control, will help produce patience in your life (Gal. 5:22). As a fruit of the Spirit, patience is something God delights to cultivate in His children. It may be only in seed form in your life right now; but if you abide in Christ, as the vine abides in the branch, you will someday bear that fruit in abundance (compare John 15:5). And as you come to rest in God, the steam will whistle out of the cooker until, at last, the pressure has been relieved.

C. Imagine the worst case. Think how a poor decision could impact you and others—not only short-term, but long-term as well. Chances are, the ramifications of that decision will be far more devastating than you could possibly predict.

D. Think of those who will be impacted by your decision. Will they be built up in character, their dignity protected? Or will their character be torn down, their integrity compromised? God is the Master Builder of personal worth and dignity. His choices reflect that. Do yours?

The story in Genesis 16 sounds as current as today's newspaper. Running ahead of the Lord is a risky way to live your life and, as we see in this passage, the results can be painful for all involved.

● Let's reread Genesis 16, focusing on the three main characters. Then, record your observations about Abram, Sarai, and Hagar in the space provided. Notice the development of their individual personality traits—Abram's passivity, Sarai's rationalization, Hagar's victimization.

Genesis 16

Abram: _____

_____

_____

_____

_____

_____

Sarai: _____

_____

_____

_____

_____

Hagar: _____

_____

_____

_____

_____

Continued on next page

Living Insights

We concluded our study with four suggestions to consider the next time you're tempted to run ahead. Did you notice their first letters spell out the acrostic WAIT? Let's give these suggestions a little more of our time and attention.

- Take a few minutes to copy the four applications onto index cards. Then commit these simple suggestions to memory by reading them over and over, preferably aloud. As humans, we're constantly tempted to hurry ahead of God, so having these helps at the forefront of our minds will be valuable in fighting off sinful tendencies.

Walk a little slower.

Ask God for patience.

Imagine the worst case.

Think of those who will be impacted by your decision.

The Joys of Walking with God

Genesis 17

Today's society thrives on big events, speed, noise, movement, and drama. But it is not hyperactivity that troubles us—it's quietness. Solitude is often considered boring, a waste of time. Mistakenly, we suppose that walking with God is a quick, easily acquired discipline. And we fail to give ourselves permission for leisure and time alone with God.

> If we try to rationalize our compulsive work habits by saying we are accomplishing things for God, then, logically, we aren't *anything* unless we are *doing* something. To make matters worse, we have taken these workaholic habits beyond the realm of work to include our personal, social, and spiritual lives as well.... And religion becomes a pattern of rules and regulations, a system that helps us tidy up our behavior, somewhat like rearranging the deck chairs on the Titanic. It allows us a better view as we go down.[1]

Abram would not understand our shallow relationships with God. His vigorous faith catapulted him into arduous foreign travel (Gen. 12–14), international military campaigns (chap. 14), a covenant with God (chap. 15)—even struggles in understanding the promise of God (chap. 16). We need to close our day-at-a-glance calendars and join the adventure for the long haul.

I. Waiting on God (Genesis 17:1–2)

Calm times are often the most spiritually significant. When the dust of our activity has settled and quiet emerges, God comes to us afresh. So it was with Abram.

A. Silent waiting (v. 1a). Thirteen years of silence lie sandwiched between chapters 16 and 17. Abram, like anybody who lives a life of trust in the Lord, experienced periods of waiting like this—sometimes long ones—between notably significant events. But God was there. He was working. He was just quiet. God is at work in our lives too—even in silent times.

B. Active reassurance (vv. 1b–2). Over a decade has elapsed since God's last visit with Abram (chap. 15). Ishmael is a teenager. Finally, when Abram's age is one year shy of the century mark, God speaks.

"I am God Almighty;
Walk before Me, and be blameless.
And I will establish My covenant between Me and you,
And I will multiply you exceedingly." (17:1b–2)

---

1. Tim Hansel, *When I Relax I Feel Guilty* (Elgin, Ill.: David C. Cook Publishing Co., 1979), p. 38.

God's commitments to Abram had never been forgotten, even though the long silence may have, at times, led him to believe otherwise.

II. Walking with God (Genesis 17:3–27)

God told Abram to "walk before Me"—the same command He gives believers today. But what does it mean to walk before, or with, God?

A. What it includes. From this passage we learn at least four ingredients of walking with God.

    1. Being quiet so God can speak (vv. 3–8). When God speaks—through His Word, through our hearts—we need to listen. When God appears to Abram, Abram closes his mouth and opens his ears. And what he hears reassures him. God not only reaffirms His covenant, He also changes Abram's name to Abraham and reminds him of a Promised Land for his descendants (vv. 2, 5, 8). Such reassurance does not come when we are on the run, but rather in the context of humility and quietness before the Lord. Perhaps the times have begun to crush in upon you and you're feeling pushed to stay busy—always on the move—to get things done. You are not alone. Maybe you feel what one author describes.

> We assume that if something can be done at all, it can be done quickly and efficiently. Our attention spans have been conditioned by thirty-second commercials....
> ... There is little enthusiasm for the patient acquisition of virtue, little inclination to sign up for a long apprenticeship in what earlier generations of Christians called holiness.[2]

Sure, you have to make a living and be involved with people. But the answer is neither a rocking chair nor a schedule that causes you to drop exhausted into bed at night. You need to stop and listen to God; otherwise, you will fail to hear His promises.

Abram Becomes Abraham

    The sky's twinkling dots—innumerable pin-bursts of light—are scanned by Abram's eyes from horizon to horizon as he tries to comprehend the number of children God promised to him (15:5). Now is God's time to set the stage for the fulfilling of that promise;

---

2. Eugene H. Peterson, *A Long Obedience in the Same Direction: Discipleship in an Instant Society* (Downers Grove, Ill.: InterVarsity Press, 1980), pp. 11–12.

and to do it, He changes the name of one of His key
actors.

> "No longer shall your name be called Abram,
> But your name shall be Abraham;
> For I will make you the father of a multitude
>   of nations." (17:5)

Abraham's new name is like a brightly lit marquee,
inviting us to view God's life-changing drama. "Exalted
father," or Abram, could be the name of any dad who
walks with God. But "father of a multitude," or Abraham,
applies only to one man—a man whose faithfulness
changed history.

God's drama continues, and it is for our benefit
that He writes the script. He delights us with an age-
old theme of just an ordinary man doing the extraor-
dinary—a simple, humble man chosen to become the
father of a great nation. Isn't it wondrous that God
takes insignificant people like you and me and uses
us beyond our greatest expectations (Ps. 113:5–9, Eph.
3:20)?

2. **Listening for specific directions** (Gen. 17:9–14). Because
Abraham listens closely to God, he learns how he and his
children will receive a mark of distinction that will set them
apart as God's special people.

> "This is My covenant, which you shall keep, be-
> tween Me and you and your descendants after
> you: every male among you shall be circumcised.
> And you shall be circumcised in the flesh of your
> foreskin; and it shall be the sign of the covenant
> between Me and you." (vv. 10–11)[3]

You, too, can learn of God's plans for your life if you'll take
time to quiet yourself before Him . . . and listen.

Our Own Special Mark

Like the Israelites, Christians also have an identify-
ing mark. The Holy Spirit is given as a seal to all who
trust Jesus as their personal Savior.

> In Him, you also, after listening to the mes-
> sage of truth, the gospel of your salvation—

---

3. Circumcision is the sign of God's covenant with Abraham. It is a physical reminder, not to
be equated with the reality of the covenant, much like the relationship between the wedding
ring and the marriage itself.

> having also believed, you were sealed in
> Him with the Holy Spirit of promise, who is
> given as a pledge of our inheritance, with
> a view to the redemption of God's own pos-
> session, to the praise of His glory. (Eph.
> 1:13–14)
>
> As a rancher brands his cattle to show ownership,
> so God seals us with the Holy Spirit to mark us as His
> own. If you have believed in the gospel, you are branded
> with God's special emblem. And once you bear His
> seal, you are entitled to enjoy His friendship forever.
> Isn't that good news?

3. **Wrestling for understanding** (Gen. 17:15–21). Sometimes
God's plan doesn't make sense to us. It certainly didn't to
Abraham. Even though God had reiterated His promises
over and over, when the time came for the first step of fulfillment—Sarai's miraculous conception of a baby boy—
Abraham collapsed in laughter at the prospect of a hundred-
year-old man and a ninety-year-old woman bearing a child.
But God patiently repeats His promise, and Abraham finally
understands. Like Abraham, we sometimes need time to
grasp God's instructions.

> **Sarai Becomes Sarah**
>
> God's promised child needed a mother, and only
> Sarai qualified. She, like Abraham, needed a name that
> proclaimed God's purpose among the nations. Her
> name would no longer be Sarai, "my princess," but
> Sarah, "princess." She would be not only the wife of
> Abraham but the princess of an entire nation. Simi-
> larly, when God finds us faithful, He extends our use-
> fulness far beyond the borders of our wildest imagi-
> nations.

4. **Obeying swiftly and thoroughly** (vv. 22–27). Walking with
God is not a passive, dreamy experience. It requires praying,
listening, and sometimes wrestling for understanding. Once
God's instructions are understood, obedience is required.
And it is Abraham's immediate and thorough obedience that
prepared him and his family to assume their national identity before the world.

B. How it improves. Our walk with God matures when we heed wise counsel. Tuck these truths in your knapsack for the days and years to come.

1. **The discipline of silence increases our sensitivity to God.** Insensitivity to God is bred by a high-paced lifestyle. Our noisy, mechanical movement needs to wind down until, at last, it is replaced with quietness. In silence we learn to change our thoughts by exposing them to God (2 Cor. 10:3–5). Cultivate a time of quietness by putting aside distractions so that your anxieties settle and your sensitivity to God increases.

2. **Understanding God's heart decreases our anxiety.** Few things are more nerve-wracking than moving on while unsure of His will and overloaded with the baggage of burdensome questions and doubts. Praying and probing to understand God's plan rewards you with stability and courage.

3. **Obeying submissively proves our humility.** Understanding God's plan provides reassurance. But only by following God's plan will we have peace . . . a peace brought by refusing pride's control and submitting to Him. Humility, as the archenemy of your pride, will then reign (James 4:6–10).

III. Responding to God

Walking with God leads to many pleasant surprises. You may have already discovered two great truths in your personal walk.

A. God delights in our obedient response. Hanani, the prophet of God, was sent to a Judean king, Asa, to rebuke him for making an alliance with a foreign king instead of relying on God for deliverance. Hanani's words are pure melody for you who have learned to trust God.

> "For the eyes of the Lord move to and fro throughout
> the earth that He may strongly support those whose
> heart is completely His." (2 Chron. 16:9a)

Isn't it wonderful to discover that your obedience inspires God's full support!

B. God relieves us of numerous disappointments. Isaiah's words to the captive Israelites reflect God's desire to keep His people from regret.

> "I am the Lord your God, who teaches you to profit,
> Who leads you in the way you should go.
> If only you had paid attention to My commandments!
> Then your well-being would have been like a river,
> And your righteousness like the waves of the sea."
> (Isa. 48:17b–18)

Life's torrential dilemmas are resolved into peaceful rivers when we obey God. He gives us His full support.

A Joyful Walk

Are you allowing quiet to command your world? Or have you failed to notice your activities creeping up and crowding out your time with God? If a harried lifestyle has you in its grip, why don't you stop right now, give yourself a treat, and read the following poem—slowly.

I wasted an hour one morning beside a mountain stream,
I seized a cloud from the sky above and fashioned myself a dream,
In the hush of the early twilight, far from the haunts of men,
I wasted a summer evening, and fashioned my dream again.
Wasted? Perhaps. Folks say so who never have walked with God,
When lanes are purple with lilacs or yellow with goldenrod.
But I have found strength for my labors in that one short evening hour.
I have found joy and contentment; I have found peace and power.
My dreaming has left me a treasure, a hope that is strong and true.
From wasted hours I have built my life and found my faith anew.[4]

Living Insights

Study One

Genesis 17 is a quiet chapter—no large splash of activity, no headline events. But what we see in it is a picture of God and His friend together.

- Sometimes reading a familiar text in an unfamiliar Bible translation brings fresh insight. See how this works for you, using a translation like the New American Standard Bible, the New International Version, or the New King James Version. You may also wish to read it in a paraphrase, like the Living Bible.

---

4. As quoted by Tim Hansel in *When I Relax I Feel Guilty,* p. 67.

Living Insights

Walking with God . . . a phrase easily tossed around by Christians. But what does it really mean to walk with God? The four suggestions we discussed in the lesson are worth further consideration. In the space provided below, write down what you think is meant by each suggestion, and evaluate how you're doing in that specific area.

Being Quiet So God Can Speak

_____

_____

_____

_____

Listening for Specific Directions

_____

_____

_____

_____

Wrestling for Understanding

_____

_____

_____

_____

Obeying Swiftly and Thoroughly

_____

_____

_____

_____

One of Those Upper-Downer Days

Genesis 18

Uppers and downers. One drug elevates, the other deflates. Taking them is like flying one moment and crashing the next.

There are days in our lives that could be described the same way. Remember the dog days of summer, long after school had recessed, when everything was thoroughly explored and there was nothing left to do? Or, in later years, remember when you came to your first job with excitement and anticipation, only to find that some days dragged with empty hours and tedious tasks? Then there are the days when you hit the road running—from the moment you get up, life is a blur of activity, full of challenges. All of us have experienced both upper and downer days ... biblical characters did as well.

Moses is a case in point. One day he arose to tend his father-in-law's sheep, as he had for years. But that morning, he saw a bush aflame and was commissioned to lead God's people out of Egypt (Exod. 3:1–4:19). For Moses, it was an upper day—an old shepherd had been appointed the leader of an entire nation.

Later, another shepherd—a young boy—took food to his brothers who were fighting Israel's battles. At the front line, he heard a Philistine giant defame the name of Israel's God. Israel's King Saul cowered faithlessly at a distance with his men while, in God's name, the indignant young shepherd, David, confronted the towering man with just a sling and a few pebbles. A single, keenly-aimed stone struck the giant in the head, and he slumped to the ground (1 Sam. 17). It was a day that would long be remembered as a definite upper.

Abraham, too, had an upper day—but his ended as a downer. It started normally, then peaked ... then plummeted.

I. The Day's Upper (Genesis 18:1–15)

Sequestered among the oaks of Mamre, Abraham has found a retreat from the day's heat (v. 1).

A. Special guests welcomed (vv. 1–8). Three men—actually the Lord and two angels[1]—walk into the shaded area where Abraham is resting.

> Now the Lord appeared to him by the oaks of Mamre, while he was sitting at the tent door in the heat of the day. And when he lifted up his eyes and looked,

---

1. This is an example of a self-manifestation of God, or a *theophany.* And for further study of angels, consult Merrill F. Unger's *Biblical Demonology,* 6th ed. (Wheaton, Ill.: Scripture Press Publications, 1965).

behold, three men were standing opposite him. (vv. 1–2a)

Abraham, in typical Near Eastern fashion, graciously receives them, offering welcome and refreshment (vv. 2–8).[2]

B. Special promise announced (vv. 9–15). As the men eat, God makes an announcement:

"I will surely return to you at this time next year; and behold, Sarah your wife shall have a son." And Sarah was listening at the tent door, which was behind him. (v. 10)

Sarah, eavesdropping from the tent, is hearing this news as well. Her reaction? Laughter (vv. 10b–12)! The visitor, not allowing her response to slide, poses a question to further punctuate the promised child's coming.

"Is anything too difficult for the Lord? At the appointed time I will return to you, at this time next year, and Sarah shall have a son." (v. 14)

Sarah steps out of the tent to defend herself. " 'I did not laugh,' " she protests (v. 15a). And immediately the Lord corrects her, " 'No, but you did laugh' " (v. 15b). This gentle rebuke may have been a downer for Sarah, but the guests brought Abraham and Sarah news they had waited twenty-five years to hear. Sarah's delivery date was set! This, as well as God's visit to these special nomads, made this day a memorable upper.

II. The Day's Downer (Genesis 18:16–21)

With the meal concluded and the message delivered, Abraham's visitors depart. He strolls with them toward Sodom (v. 16).

A. A compassionate monologue (vv. 17–21). The Lord contemplates sharing another item of news with Abraham.

"Shall I hide from Abraham what I am about to do, since Abraham will surely become a great and mighty nation, and in him all the nations of the earth will be blessed? For I have chosen him, in order that he may command his children and his household after him to keep the way of the Lord by doing righteousness and justice; in order that the Lord may bring upon Abraham what He has spoken about him." (vv. 17–19)

---

2. Roland de Vaux vividly portrays the importance of nomadic hospitality: "Hospitality . . . is a necessity of life in the desert, but among the nomads this necessity has become a virtue, and a most highly esteemed one." From *Ancient Israel: Social Institutions* (New York, N.Y.: McGraw-Hill Book Co., 1965), vol. 1, p. 10. In the Old Testament, recall Laban's hospitality (Gen. 24:28–32) and Lot's (19:1–8), and, in the New Testament, the matter of entertaining angels unaware (Heb. 13:2).

God decides to confide in Abraham . . . and the downer begins.

> And the Lord said, "The outcry of Sodom and Gomor-
> rah is indeed great, and their sin is exceedingly grave.
> I will go down now, and see if they have done entirely
> according to its outcry, which has come to Me; and
> if not, I will know." (vv. 20–21)

Metropolitan Mania

The twin cities of Sodom and Gomorrah sang a duet of destruction whose dissonant sound reached heaven. Does the corruption of *our* cities cry out to God? Does murder . . . rape . . . robbery . . . the filth of our minds create a clashing chord that is heard in heaven? Examine your *mental* metropolis. Is it in concert with the world's mania? Or is it harmonizing in the spirit of the "Hallelujah Chorus"?

B. A passionate dialogue (vv. 22–33). The two angels depart for Sodom and Gomorrah while Abraham is "still standing before the Lord" (v. 22). Compassion for Lot and his family has seized his mind. He knows the Lord well enough to realize the cities are as good as gone, and he is compelled to intercede for his nephew.

> "Wilt Thou indeed sweep away the righteous with the
> wicked? Suppose there are fifty righteous within the
> city; wilt Thou indeed sweep it away and not spare
> the place for the sake of the fifty righteous who are
> in it?" (vv. 23–24)

The Lord answers agreeably,

> "If I find in Sodom fifty righteous within the city, then
> I will spare the whole place on their account." (v. 26)

Abraham is not satisfied. He continues to appeal to God's mercy, persistently petitioning God to consider the righteous in the city. God consents to cancel the sentence if He finds as few as ten righteous people (vv. 27–32). But Sodom's potential fate plays with Abraham's mood like a downer, because he suspects that not even ten righteous people will be found.

III. Getting a Grip on Those Upper-Downer Days

We've all had roller coaster days; none of us are exempt from those hair-raising rides. Abraham's experience gives us clues to brace ourselves for both the uppers and the downers.

A. Watch for God. The Lord appeared to Abraham in a subtle way, without announcement. Learn to look for God in everyday settings. Listen for His voice in your conversations with others, and look for His fingerprints in the creation around you. Pause to hear Him as you read Scripture and as you sing spiritual songs. Such common occurrences can reflect the Lord's plans (Rom. 1:20). Keep your eyes, ears, and heart open to Him.

B. Walk with God. Abraham's stroll with God taught him God's plan. As you walk with Him, you, too, will fall into rhythm with His step—and move in the direction He is going (Col. 1:9–10).

C. Talk to God. Abraham felt comfortable enough in the Lord's presence to contend for a sinful city. God cares about our concerns and hears our requests as well. Do you forfeit peace of mind because you fail to take your worries to God? For some helpful advice, see Philippians 4:6–7.

D. Wait on God. His plans are greater than our pleas (Isa. 55:8–9). Abraham's concern for Lot moved God to mercy. God honored Abraham's request, but not in the way Abraham expected. God sees so much farther, understands so much more, than His children do . . . and those who wait on Him experience His peace (26:3).

 Living Insights

Study One ▬▬▬▬▬▬▬▬▬▬▬▬▬▬▬▬▬▬▬▬▬▬▬▬▬

Not even ten righteous people could be found in Sodom. What about in your town? Are you different from the unrighteous of your day? What makes you stand out from the crowd? Think about it, and then record your thoughts in the space below.

What Distinguishes Me from My Godless Society?

_____

_____

_____

_____

_____

_____

_____

_____

Continued on next page

_____

_____

_____

_____

🌺 *Living Insights*

Study Two ▬▬▬▬▬▬▬▬▬▬▬▬▬▬▬▬▬▬▬▬▬▬▬▬

Genesis 18 is a record of one of those upper-downer days. It started high—with real excitement. But it ended full of sorrow. Let's look at some of the action that took place.

- One of the best ways to examine the action in this passage is to take a closer look at the verbs. As you read through Genesis 18, pick out fifteen or twenty action words in the text. Write down why you feel each verb is key to the story.

Genesis 18	
Verb	Significance

Understanding the Dynamics of Prayer

Numbers 11:1–33, Genesis 18–19, Judges 16:26–30

Many of us struggle to understand prayer when our words seem to bounce off ceilings or simply float in space. And sometimes we feel so self-conscious when we address God that we can't conceive of having the kind of friendship Abraham had with Him. All our inadequacies automatically raise a barrier when we are alone with God. However, as our maturity level rises, we learn how adequate Jesus is to bridge the gulf between us and God . . . and we become more bold before Him, understanding more fully our complete acceptance in Jesus (Heb. 4:14, 16).

Abraham was not a superior human with unique access to God; he merely responded to God's call by faith (11:8). And God, in turn, became his friend.

"I have selected this man to be my friend. I also want him as a partner. He will have a role in my plans. Moreover, though I know he will keep my precepts and teach them to his children, I want him to be more than a yes man. I want him to be a true partner, sharing fully in those projects he will have a part in."[1]

God's intimacy with Abraham is duplicated many times over in people who understand their spiritual roots and stand confidently before the Lord in prayer (Eph. 1:4–7, 3:20).

As you grow in your understanding of prayer, timidity before God will turn to humble confidence.

I. The Ingredients of Prayer

Prayer includes two dynamics: the petition itself, and the motive behind it. The petition is the *content* of prayer—without which prayer cannot be answered.

You do not have because you do not ask. (James 4:2c)

Yet an earnest prayer made for improper reasons negates the whole purpose of communication with God.

You ask and do not receive, because you ask with wrong motives. (v. 3a)

Let's analyze the fine balance between petitions and motives so we can better understand the role of prayer in our lives.

---

1. John White, *Daring to Draw Near: People in Prayer* (Downers Grove, Ill.: Inter-Varsity Press, 1977), p. 17.

II. God's Responses to Prayer

How God responds to our prayers depends many times on us—what's going on inside of us and what our circumstances are.

A. He may say yes to the petition but no to the desire (Num. 11:1–33). When Moses led the Israelites out of captivity, God miraculously fed them manna from heaven. But the ungrateful Israelites grumbled and complained, comparing the monotonous manna to the main dishes they had enjoyed in Egypt. Wistful memories of savory meals made their mouths water for meat and potatoes as they lost their appetite for God's food. Moses threw up his hands and turned to God. "What have I done to deserve these people, Lord? Where am I gonna get meat for them out here in the desert?" Moses was displeased with them; God was displeased. But still God honored their request. And the next day the Israelites were stubbing their toes on quail. You can almost hear God's exasperated sigh as He answers Moses:

"And say to the people, 'Consecrate yourselves for tomorrow, and you shall eat meat; for you have wept in the ears of the Lord, saying, "Oh that someone would give us meat to eat! For we were well-off in Egypt." Therefore the Lord will give you meat and you shall eat.' " (v. 18)

God may grant requests that are improperly motivated, but we won't find satisfaction in their fulfillment. Take note of the rest of God's message to the Israelites.

" 'You shall eat, not one day, nor two days, nor five days, nor ten days, nor twenty days, but a whole month, until it comes out of your nostrils and becomes loathsome to you; because you have rejected the Lord who is among you and have wept before Him, saying, "Why did we ever leave Egypt?" ' " (v. 19)

God's anger was boiling. The Israelites not only became sick of meat; they became sick from it.

So He gave them their request,
But sent a wasting disease among them. (Ps. 106:15)

The King James version says it another way; He "sent leanness into their soul." God will sometimes allow our wrong desires to be fulfilled. But the result is like eating spoiled food.

Leanness in Our Souls

Leanness diseased the souls of the Israelites, and it can disease our souls as well. For example, a lonely, single

---

70

person may leap heedlessly into an unwise marriage . . . and find the relationship as lean and unsatisfying as unending days of quail. Or a young person may pray for prosperity and receive it . . . but find that satisfaction evaporates with every selfishly spent dollar. Desires that compromise godly values are costly, and the fattening fruits of greedy indulgence starve souls.

B. God may say no to our petitions but yes to our desires (Gen. 18–19). When Abraham learned of God's plan to destroy the corrupt cities of Sodom and Gomorrah (18:20–21), he petitioned the Lord to save Sodom. A piece of Abraham's heart was in that city, for his nephew Lot lived there, along with Lot's entire family—a family that was in jeopardy of being destroyed through guilt by association. Abraham's petition was denied—but his concern for Lot was answered. God did not save Sodom—but He did deliver Lot (19:15–16). While we may misstate our requests, God understands their intent (Rom. 8:26).

┌─ *A Soldier's Prayer* ─────────────────────────────

"I asked God for strength that I might achieve.
I was made weak that I might learn humbly
　　to obey.

I asked God for health that I might do greater
　　things.
I was given infirmity that I might do better
　　things.

I asked for riches that I might be happy.
I was given poverty that I might be wise.

I asked for power that I might have the praise
　　of men.
I was given weakness that I might feel the
　　need of God.

I asked for all things that I might enjoy life.
I was given life that I might enjoy all things.

I got nothing that I asked for
but everything I had hoped for . . .

> Almost despite myself my unspoken prayers
> were answered.
>
> I am among all men most richly blessed."[2]

C. God may answer yes to both our petitions and our desires (Judg. 16:26–30). Samson served as a judge during the dark ages of decadence in Israel's history (13:5–7, 15:20). His great strength made him a bulwark of defense against the Philistines—until he fell for the Philistine temptress, Delilah, who pestered him until he told her the secret of his strength (16:16–17). Delilah used that knowledge against him (vv. 18–20), and for the first time Samson experienced physical weakness. The Philistines capitalized on the moment. But in gouging his eyes out, chaining, and imprisoning him, they were only preparing Samson for his greatest triumph (vv. 21–22). A Philistine victory festival was called to give praise to their god, Dagon, for the demise of Samson, whom they called "the destroyer of our country" (v. 24). As the festival reached its apex, the people demanded to see the defeated man who had disrupted their families (vv. 23–27). The place was brimming with Philistine dignitaries. Samson was brought and positioned in the middle of the room between two supporting pillars. While his enemies ridiculed, he prayed,

> "O Lord God, please remember me and please strengthen me just this time, O God, that I may at once be avenged of the Philistines for my two eyes." (v. 28)

Then Samson bent his shoulders to the task of pulling the pillars down (v. 29). As the supports began to crumble, he made one last request, "Let me die with the Philistines!" The building collapsed, and "the dead whom he killed at his death were more than those whom he killed in his life" (v. 30). God granted both Samson's request and his desire. God's approval flows when our purposes are knit with our Father's heart. "The effective prayer of a righteous man can accomplish much" (James 5:16b).[3]

D. God may say no to both our petitions and our desires. There are several reasons why God sometimes responds to both our requests and our motives with a resounding no.

---

2. By an unknown Confederate soldier, as quoted in Tim Hansel's *When I Relax I Feel Guilty* (Elgin, Ill.: David C. Cook Publishing Co., 1979), p. 89.

3. Elijah is the example of the righteous man. Read 1 Kings 17:1 and 18:1, 42 for a background to James 5:17–18.

1. **We ourselves may be the cause.** Our attitudes can be bricks in a wall that blocks us from God and muffles our requests. One brick is unconfessed sin.

> If I regard wickedness in my heart,
> The Lord will not hear. (Ps. 66:18)

Another brick is an unclear conscience. If you've offended someone without asking forgiveness, or if you're letting bitterness sour your heart, God will not answer (Matt. 5:23). Hypocrisy and pride cement the bricks in place (6:5). Layer upon layer, the attitudes stack up: selfishness and wrong motives (James 4:3); faltering faith (Mark 11:24); lack of compassion (Prov. 21:13); even an unhealthy relationship between husband and wife (1 Pet. 3:7). It's a formidable wall, isn't it? But with a clean heart, humbled before God, that wall will come tumbling down (1 John 1:9).

2. **God may have another plan.** Even when our hearts are clean—even when our pleas are pleasing—sometimes even then God says no. Not to be mean. Not just to wield His power. But because He has a better way.[4]

> "For My thoughts are not your thoughts,
> Neither are your ways My ways," declares the
> Lord.
> "For as the heavens are higher than the earth,
> So are My ways higher than your ways,
> And My thoughts than your thoughts."
> (Isa. 55:8–9)

III. God's Answers to Prayer

When our hearts are clean as we pray, God never fails to respond.

A. Sometimes God says yes. These are magnificent moments when our petition and desires match His purposes (1 John 5:14–15).

B. Sometimes God says no. It's hard to accept this response, but we may be assured that God's plans are for our good (Jer. 29:11).

C. Sometimes God says wait. It's easy to confuse this with a no. But we are challenged to keep asking until the wait becomes a definite yes or no (Matt. 7:7–8).

Continued on next page

---

4. God may be teaching you a valuable lesson (for example, see 2 Cor. 12:9–10) or using you as an object lesson for others as He did Hosea, Ezekiel, and Jeremiah (Hos 1:2–11, Ezek. 5, Jer. 16).

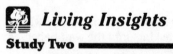

Living Insights

Prayer is one of the greatest privileges of the Christian life. Let's broaden our study of prayer by looking at some other passages that deal with this subject.

- With the help of a Bible concordance, look up *pray, praying,* and *prayer.* Choose several of the listed passages to study. Record the references and the lessons you learn.

Prayer	
Verses	Observations

Living Insights

Perhaps you discovered something new about prayer in our study; perhaps you saw some old truths in a new way. Now let's really bring them to life.

- Take some time now to pray. As you talk with the Lord, bring your petitions honestly before Him. Trust His response as He answers with a yes, no, or wait, realizing that the answer will come in good time. You can rest assured that He knows what He's doing!

When the Cesspool Overflows

Genesis 19:1–14

An ounce of prevention is worth a pound of correction—it fends off costly mistakes before they happen. For example, picture a road winding up a mountain. It has a sharp curve and a cliff that slices away to the valley floor below. The highway department has two options for dealing with this hazard. They can build a clinic in the valley staffed with qualified medical personnel to take care of accident victims, or they can strategically post signs that warn, Danger—Curve Ahead—10 MPH. The signs would be preventative solutions, while the clinic would be purely corrective.

Although God is on hand to help us when we crash, His Word is billboarded with warnings so that we can avoid dangerous mistakes.

I. Warnings of Contamination

As we journey through the Old and New Testaments, we find ourselves screeching to a halt in the face of boldly painted Do Not Enter signs that guard the entrance to certain relationships.

A. In the Old Testament. The Israelites, in Joshua 23, were warned to keep their distance from enemy nations—specifically, not to intermarry with them (vv. 6–8, 11–13). And in 1 Kings 11, we see why. Solomon ignored God's warning and helped himself to generous portions of passion with women from forbidden countries. He married some and kept others as concubines; but, in the end, it was the women who had their way.

> For it came about when Solomon was old, his wives turned his heart away after other gods; and his heart was not wholly devoted to the Lord his God, as the heart of David his father had been. (v. 4)

Mixed Marriages?

God forbade the Israelites to intermarry with people from other races or nationalities . . . but His objection was not to the color of their skin, the shape of their features, or the texture of their hair. His objection was to the ungodly hearts of heathen nations. The intent of His instruction is clearer in the New Testament.

> Do not be bound together with unbelievers; for what partnership have righteousness and lawlessness, or what fellowship has light with darkness? Or what harmony has Christ with Belial, or what has a believer in common with an unbeliever? (2 Cor. 6:14–15)

> The idea of being "bound together" is shown in the Old Testament law that prohibited crossbreeding of different kinds of animals (Lev. 19:19a). Deuteronomy 22:10 states, " 'You shall not plow with an ox and a donkey together.' " In those days plows were pulled by two animals secured in the same yoke. Two different kinds of animals wouldn't have possessed equal pulling power, so they were not yoked together.
>
> Just as an ox and a donkey could not pull together in the same yoke, so a believer cannot pull harmoniously with an unbeliever in the yoke of marriage.

In Proverbs, God warns us against another contaminating involvement—associating with gossips.

> He who goes about as a slanderer reveals secrets,
> Therefore do not associate with a gossip. (20:19)

Whose reputation hasn't been scratched and dented by reckless gossips? Likewise, who hasn't been injured by people given to anger? Proverbs 22:24–25 cautions us to stay away from hot-tempered people as well.[1] God's instructions are for our good. Not only does He want to help us avoid the pain that can come from wrong associations, He wants us to avoid picking up the faults of those involved.

B. In the New Testament. The apostle Paul goes on to post God's warning signs about harmful associations.

> But actually, I wrote to you not to associate with any so-called brother if he should be an immoral person, or covetous, or an idolater, or a reviler, or a drunkard, or a swindler—not even to eat with such a one. (1 Cor. 5:11)

When you choose your friends wisely, you honor God—and protect yourself.

> Do not be deceived: "Bad company corrupts good morals." (15:33)

Even great men of God are susceptible to moral erosion. Remember Lot?

II. A Classic Example of Moral Deterioration

Lot had observed Abraham's success in business and in social relationships, and he'd watched him during stressful times as well as joyful times. But he forgot that these benefits were fruits of Abraham's relationship with God; and, in Sodom, Lot turned his energies to the

---

1. Compare the New Testament verses in James 1:19–20.

pursuit of wealth and social status instead of to his walk with the Lord. So he stayed in Sodom, even though wickedness was a hallmark of the region (Gen. 13:13), making his home there (14:12). But why? Because it's hard to lure a mouse out of a corncrib as long as there is corn. In our passage, we find Lot in the silo, feeding on the grain of finance and position while his moral life is starving. Wealthy and complacent, he doesn't comprehend how putrid Sodom's moral sewage has become to God (18:20).

A. Lot in the wicked city (19:1). Entering Sodom, we find Lot at the city's gate, a place of prominence where legal, civil, and business transactions are conducted.[2] While acting as an official in city affairs, he's approached by two visitors.

> Now the two angels came to Sodom in the evening as Lot was sitting in the gate of Sodom. When Lot saw them, he rose to meet them and bowed down with his face to the ground.

B. Lot with heavenly guests (vv. 2–3). Though Lot is entrenched in Sodom's affairs, he is not completely naive about its moral condition. When the visitors arrive, presumably unaware of Sodom's despicable state, Lot urges them to spend the night in the safety of his home.[3]

> Yet he urged them strongly, so they turned aside to him and entered his house; and he prepared a feast for them, and baked unleavened bread, and they ate. (v. 3)

Lot had no idea that this evening would be recorded as one of the most sordid in all of biblical history. What began with hospitality would end in terror.

C. Lot among immoral citizens (vv. 4–11). Word gets out that there are male visitors at Lot's house, and Sodom's homosexual citizens, young and old, are drawn to his doorstep.

> Before they lay down, the men of the city, the men of Sodom, surrounded the house, both young and old, all the people from every quarter; and they called to Lot and said to him, "Where are the men who came to you tonight? Bring them out to us that we may have relations with them." (vv. 4–5)

---

2. Very likely, the city's leaders favored Lot because his uncle, Abraham, had liberated Sodom from the Mesopotamian kings (Gen. 14:16–17).

3. These are the same "men" in Genesis 18:22, and their angelic nature may not yet have been revealed to Lot.

Homosexuality's perversion surrounded Lot's house.[4] Vile men, minds aflame with lust, waited for Lot's response. It's important to remember that, weak and passive though Lot was, he remained a believer. He struggled with his neighbors' corrupt practices; the New Testament even says that he was

> oppressed by the sensual conduct of unprincipled men (for by what he saw and heard that righteous man, while living among them, felt his righteous soul tormented day after day with their lawless deeds). (2 Pet. 2:7b–8)

So Lot steps outside and proposes a compromise (Gen. 19:6). But the compromise merely reveals his failure to protect his own children.

> "Now behold, I have two daughters who have not had relations with man; please let me bring them out to you, and do to them whatever you like; only do nothing to these men, inasmuch as they have come under the shelter of my roof." (v. 8)

Was this a legitimate offer, or just a ploy?[5] It didn't seem to matter to these abhorrent men. They forcefully rejected Lot's offer and turned their vile intentions upon gaining access to the men inside.

> But they said, "Stand aside." Furthermore, they said, "This one came in as an alien, and already he is acting like a judge; now we will treat you worse than them." So they pressed hard against Lot and came near to break the door. (v. 9)

Lot was helplessly outnumbered, but the angelic visitors came to the rescue by blinding his assailants.

> But the men reached out their hands and brought Lot into the house with them, and shut the door. And they struck the men who were at the doorway of the house with blindness, both small and great, so that they wearied themselves trying to find the doorway. (vv. 10–11)

---

4. Homosexuality is condemned by God as a perversion (see Lev. 20:13, Rom. 1:26–27, 1 Cor. 6:9–10, 1 Tim. 1:9–10).

5. H. C. Leupold summarizes the opposing views of C. F. Keil and F. Delitzsch, and Martin Luther. Keil and Delitzsch believed Lot tried to "avoid sin by sin" at a time when "an exaggerated emphasis on hospitality prevailed." Luther believed Lot was being shrewd and expected the citizens to reject his offer. Leupold himself feels Delitzsch is closer to the truth because Scripture implies that Lot failed to comprehend the depth of Sodom's depravity. See *Exposition of Genesis* (1942; reprint, Grand Rapids, Mich.: Baker Book House, 1965), vol. 1, pp. 559–60.

D. Lot and his indifferent family (vv. 12–14). The riotous atmosphere becomes suddenly somber as the angelic visitors share their mission and concern with Lot.

> "Whom else have you here? A son-in-law, and your sons, and your daughters, and whomever you have in the city, bring them out of the place; for we are about to destroy this place, because their outcry has become so great before the Lord that the Lord has sent us to destroy it." (vv. 12–13)

In spite of the urgency of the situation, Lot's warning to his family falls on unbelieving ears.

> And Lot went out and spoke to his sons-in-law, who were to marry his daughters, and said, "Up, get out of this place, for the Lord will destroy the city." But he appeared to his sons-in-law to be jesting. (v. 14)

"You're joking," his sons-in-law replied. Like gums injected with novocaine, their sensitivity to perversion had been deadened.

III. Developing and Maintaining Godly Convictions

Lot had failed to instill in his family the convictions that would keep them from building a moral system around cultural traditions.[6] Since even strong, godly convictions can be hard to uphold, let's clarify how we can develop and maintain them.

A. Convictions must be clearly established before God, or they will be subtly twisted before men. All of us are flooded daily with a sea of information. Unless you know what you believe—unless you've made commitments before God—the winds of opinion will sway you.

B. Convictions must be modeled in the home, or they will be compromised in the street. Children have no greater influence than their parents—for good or evil. The home, life's laboratory, is where values are modeled and molded (Deut. 6:4–7, Prov. 22:6). Parents can't seal off their children from the influence of the world, but they can give their children tools for evaluating what they see, hear, and feel (1:2–5).

C. Convictions must make sense to us personally, or they will mean nothing to us publicly. Hand-me-down beliefs may look fine in church—at least on the surface—but they tatter and tear when put to real use. Explore God's Word; develop convictions that are truly yours . . . and you won't easily back down in the face of temptation.

---

6. A *conviction* is a belief in a principle of life that encompasses personal integrity, morality, and faith.

Living Insights

Deep, strong, firmly established beliefs regarding integrity, morality, and faith . . . we call them *convictions*. Scripture is clear about the necessity of maintaining them. Let's explore what it says.

● Our study closes with three timeless principles on maintaining convictions, which are listed in the chart below. Look for Bible verses that support each statement. Start with verses that come to mind, then use the cross-referencing available in a study Bible or topical Bible.

Maintaining Convictions	
Principles	Verses
Convictions must be clearly established before God, or they will be subtly twisted before men.	
Convictions must be modeled in the home, or they will be compromised in the street.	
Convictions must make sense to us personally, or they will mean nothing to us publicly.	

Living Insights

The lesson we just studied teaches us the tragedy of shaky convictions. If we will drive our stakes deep into the ground of Scripture and apply the principles in Study One, we should have a better handle on the importance of sound personal beliefs and how they're developed.

● How would you advise someone to begin establishing convictions? Maybe that "someone" is a son or daughter, disciple or employee. Write this person a letter expressing what you know about building these beliefs. The letter doesn't have to be mailed, but the process of putting your thoughts into words can prove valuable to you.

A Wail of Two Cities
Genesis 19:15–29

We who seek God must come to grips with His majesty. His attributes—power, wisdom, faithfulness, goodness, love, holiness, patience, justice, to name a few—describe His majesty. They give us a glimpse of all that He is. No other pursuit is more noble than seeking to know God. How we personally understand and embrace Him is the single most revealing aspect about our lives.

Abraham's nephew Lot knew something of God. He relied solely on God's patience and mercy, His long-suffering in the face of evil. But Lot lacked understanding of how God's holiness determines His response to sustained evil. This study is a lesson in God's severity, heard in the wail of Sodom and Gomorrah.

I. A Theological Principle We Tend to Forget

As we learn about God's ways, we see the duality of His patience and His severity.

A. The fact. God is long-suffering, but His patience does have a limit. The story of the Flood in Genesis 6 is a case in point. God's holiness was affronted by the immorality that covered the earth. However, He was not quick to execute judgment. Before He let loose the downpour of His wrath, He withheld His severity 120 years while Noah built an ark to save a righteous remnant (v. 3, 7:13–23). One hundred twenty years of grace, forty days and nights of righteous anger. Clearly, while God's severity is to be respected, His merciful patience is like a cloud filled with blessing.

> But Thou, O Lord, art a God merciful and gracious,
> Slow to anger and abundant in lovingkindness and
> truth. (Ps. 86:15)

Patience and Justice

We appreciate God's patience when *we* have done wrong, don't we? But that same quality frustrates us when *others* wrong us. Then we become impatient, wanting to take things into our own hands. Yet Scripture urges us not to take our own revenge but to "leave room for the wrath of God" (Rom. 12:19). Learning from the prayer of the psalmist, we can rest in the Lord's justice.

> O Lord, God of vengeance;
> God of vengeance, shine forth!
> Rise up, O Judge of the earth;
> Render recompense to the proud.
> How long shall the wicked, O Lord,

> How long shall the wicked exult?...
> He who planted the ear, does He not hear?
> He who formed the eye, does He not see?
> He who chastens the nations, will He not
> rebuke,
> Even He who teaches man knowledge?
> The Lord knows the thoughts of man....
> But the Lord has been my stronghold,
> And my God the rock of my refuge.
> And He has brought back their wickedness
> upon them,
> And will destroy them in their evil;
> The Lord our God will destroy them.
> (Ps. 94:1–3, 9–11a, 22–23; see also Pss. 37, 73)

B. The reason. While God is patient and long-suffering, His holy character cannot allow iniquity to rule and reign supreme, polluting the earth indefinitely. He does not wink at sin. To do so would fuel the cynic's doubts about the goodness, justice, and power of God. Rather, the Lord *vindicates* His people (Deut. 32:36)—delivering, avenging, and exonerating the righteous. Remember, God's love for man, whose deadly sin could not be ignored, cost God a great price ... the life of His Son. You may be sure His righteousness *will* be satisfied in His time and way.

The God Who Vindicates You

What a comfort, child of God, to know that whatever comes against you, God will be there to stand by you. Count on it. Seek Him, and you can count on Him to resolve those hostilities. As Proverbs 16:7 says,

> When a man's ways are pleasing to the Lord,
> He makes even his enemies to be at peace with
> him.

II. A Historical Account We Cannot Deny

The outcries from Sodom and Gomorrah weighed heavily on God's heart.

> And the Lord said, "The outcry of Sodom and Gomorrah
> is indeed great, and their sin is exceedingly grave." (Gen.
> 18:20)

Those cries came daily, finally tipping the scales so that the full weight of God's severity came down to crush those wicked cities.

"For we [God's angels] are about to destroy this place, because their outcry has become so great before the Lord that the Lord has sent us to destroy it." (19:13)

A. Grace: an answer to prayer (vv. 15–22). Remember Abraham's prayer for Lot?

> And Abraham came near and said, "Wilt Thou indeed sweep away the righteous with the wicked?...Far be it from Thee to do such a thing, to slay the righteous with the wicked, so that the righteous and the wicked are treated alike. Far be it from Thee! Shall not the Judge of all the earth deal justly?" (18:23, 25)

Though ten righteous people could not be found in the city, God graciously gives Lot an opportunity to flee.

> And when morning dawned, the angels urged Lot, saying, "Up, take your wife and your two daughters, who are here, lest you be swept away in the punishment of the city." (19:15)

Yet Lot drags his feet.

> But he hesitated. So the men seized his hand and the hand of his wife and the hands of his daughters, for the compassion of the Lord was upon him; and they brought him out, and put him outside the city. And it came about when they had brought them outside, that one said, "Escape for your life! Do not look behind you, and do not stay anywhere in the valley; escape to the mountains, lest you be swept away." (vv. 16–17)

The angels are on a mission from God—a mission not only to destroy Sodom and Gomorrah but to save Lot and his family. Lot, however, doesn't like being rushed out of town on such short notice. So he proposes an alternate plan.

> But Lot said to them, "Oh no, my lords! Now behold, your servant has found favor in your sight, and you have magnified your lovingkindness, which you have shown me by saving my life; but I cannot escape to the mountains, lest the disaster overtake me and I die; now behold, this town is near enough to flee to, and it is small. Please, let me escape there (is it not small?) that my life may be saved." And he said to him, "Behold, I grant you this request also, not to overthrow the town of which you have spoken. Hurry, escape there, for I cannot do anything until you arrive there." Therefore the name of the town was called Zoar. (vv. 18–22)

One Old Testament scholar wrote this about Lot's hesitancy:

> It almost taxes the reader's patience to bear with this long-winded plea at a moment of such extreme danger. Lot appreciated but little what was being done for him.[1]

Nevertheless, Lot's request is granted and carried out, reflecting God's care for his safety.

B. Judgment: a consequence of sin (vv. 23–26). Lot escapes with his wife and two daughters just in time.

> The sun had risen over the earth when Lot came to Zoar. Then the Lord rained on Sodom and Gomorrah brimstone and fire from the Lord out of heaven, and He overthrew those cities, and all the valley, and all the inhabitants of the cities, and what grew on the ground. (vv. 23–25)

Burning sulphur and asphalt now rain upon all the inhabitants of the plain, obliterating all living things within the God-appointed perimeter of destruction.[2] Yet in the midst of the disaster, another member of Lot's family resists the angel's advice. The warning had been clear, " 'Escape for your life! Do not look behind you' " (v. 17).

> But his wife, from behind him, looked back; and she became a pillar of salt. (v. 26)

And there she stood, a monument to the grip that Sodom's lifestyle had on her.

> The overwhelming of Lot's wife as the molten materials of the explosion rained down on her . . . captures in a single picture the fate of those who turn back.[3]

A Woman of Salt

What a succinct reminder to all who hesitate to make a clear-cut, thorough break from evil. Jesus Himself reminds us: " 'Remember Lot's wife' " (Luke 17:32).

By the way, her family never saw it happen. They had obeyed the warning about not looking behind them. Not until later did they realize what had occurred. There's a definite lesson here about running from wrong: even if others don't, you do it!

---

1. H. C. Leupold, *Exposition of Genesis* (Grand Rapids, Mich.: Baker Book House, 1942), vol. 1, p. 566.

2. For further discussion on the destruction of Sodom and Gomorrah, see H. C. Leupold's *Exposition of Genesis,* vol. 1, pp. 568–71.

3. Derek Kidner, *Genesis: An Introduction and Commentary* (1967; reprint, Downers Grove, Ill.: Inter-Varsity Press, 1973), p. 135.

C. Reflection: a lesson on holiness (Gen. 19:27–29). Coming now to verses 27 through 29, we are suddenly brought across the burning valley and returned to the hill near the oaks of Mamre.

> Now Abraham arose early in the morning and went to the place where he had stood before the Lord; and he looked down toward Sodom and Gomorrah, and toward all the land of the valley, and he saw, and behold, the smoke of the land ascended like the smoke of a furnace. Thus it came about, when God destroyed the cities of the valley, that God remembered Abraham, and sent Lot out of the midst of the overthrow, when He overthrew the cities in which Lot lived.

How Abraham's heart must have ached for Lot. What compassion he felt for his nephew... yet what helplessness. The vast volumes of smoke must have been frightening as they billowed ominously above the ruins. The smoke carried a clear message: I am the Lord! Vengeance is Mine! Be holy... for I am holy!

III. Some Personal Certainties

Below are several facts we can trust as we consider the patience and severity of God in our own lives.

A. God is still a God of holiness. God's character has not changed. Neither have His standards (Ps. 102:27; compare Heb. 13:8). As He was in Abraham's day, so He is in ours. He is *still* grieved by sin, and He *still* gets angry when it is flaunted in His face.

B. Depravity has not been improved over the centuries. Perhaps it's more sophisticated or handled with greater finesse, but sin is still sin. And it's still going to be judged by God.

C. God's grace is still our only hope for survival. This is good news for any bad-news situation. But it is often rejected, as with Lot's sons-in-law. Or not completely embraced, as with Lot's wife. Yet God's patience allows us time to take hold of His grace (Rom. 9:22–23, Eph. 2:8–9). Deliverance hangs on the wire of God's patience—which is durable enough to lift the most heavily burdened sinner into the forgiving arms of God.

> Behold then the kindness and severity of God; to those who fell, severity, but to you, God's kindness. (Rom. 11:22a)

Continued on next page

Living Insights

This lesson has done much to remind us of an important theological truth: God is long-suffering, but His patience has a limit. Let's return to Genesis 19 for a look at the destruction of Sodom and Gomorrah.

- Write out Genesis 19:15–29 in your own words. As you paraphrase, try to bring out the emotions of the characters and discover new meanings from the passage.

My Paraphrase of Genesis 19:15–29

_____

_____

_____

_____

_____

_____

_____

_____

_____

_____

_____

_____

_____

_____

_____

_____

_____

_____

_____

🐾 Living Insights

We often learn our deepest lessons during times of silent reflection after a calamity. The three reminders that close this message are important truths for all Christians. Let's make them part of our lives.

● Commit these three statements to memory. One helpful method is writing each of them on an index card and reading them aloud, over and over. Soon you'll realize that you are depending less on the card and more on your memory. Ask God to help you use these statements to deepen your walk with Him.

—God is still a God of holiness.
—Depravity has not been improved over the centuries.
—God's grace is still our only hope for survival.

Ultimate Indecency
Genesis 19:30–38

The moral values in America are like shifting sand or eroding soil. The family feels this erosion, yet often without understanding why or how it happens. And the results of shifting standards are devastating.

> When the morals of society are upset, the family is the first to suffer.... The breaking up of a home does not often make headlines, but it eats like termites at the structure of the nation.[1]

Moral erosion is not obvious or loud or quick. But it is consistent and destructive. You may be among those who wonder how secure the supports of *your* family really are. Let's take a closer look at your home and see if it exhibits the signs of a deteriorating family.

I. Signs of a Deteriorating Family

Former Harvard professor Dr. Carle Zimmerman connects the deterioration of various cultures to the decline of their family unit. He discovered that anti-family sentiment begins with the educators, the wealthy, and the governing classes. Their subtle influence shifts society's values away from the family, and eventually the debunked family itself contributes to the moral decline of civilization.[2] All it takes is a small eddy of anti-family sentiment lapping against the home to draw it into a whirlpool that pulls civilization downward. Here are several signs that mark the deterioration of a family.[3]

—Marriage loses its sacredness... is frequently broken by divorce.
—Traditional meaning of the marriage ceremony is lost.
—Feminist movements abound.
—Increased public disrespect for parents and authority in general.
—Acceleration of juvenile delinquency, promiscuity, and rebellion.
—Refusal of people with traditional marriages to accept family responsibilities.
—Growing desire for and acceptance of adultery.
—Increasing interest in and spread of sexual perversions and sex-related crimes.

When human beings are no longer viewed as sacred, every perversion imaginable develops. What are listed above as signs of deterioration are actually symptoms of abandonment from God's design.

---

1. Billy Graham, *World Aflame* (Garden City, N.Y.: Doubleday and Co., 1965), p. 23.

2. Carle C. Zimmerman, *Family and Civilization* (New York, N.Y.: Harper and Brothers, 1947), pp. 703–4.

3. Charles R. Swindoll, *The Quest for Character* (Portland, Oreg.: Multnomah Press, 1987), p. 90, as paraphrased from Carle C. Zimmerman, *Family and Civilization.*

II. A Case of a Deteriorating Family

Family deterioration is not excluded from the pages of Scripture. Lot's family is an infamous example.

A. Historical circumstances. Two words will suffice to give the historical context of Lot's family: Sodom and Gomorrah. No two more notorious cities could be found. These were cities of shameless wickedness...blatant immorality...unchecked homosexuality...aggressive, brutal perversion. When two guests—who were actually angels—tried to deliver Lot from the impending destruction of Sodom, he and his family dug their heels in. Obviously, Sodom's lifestyle had taken root. Notice first the response of Lot's sons-in-law.

> And Lot went out and spoke to his sons-in-law, who were to marry his daughters, and said, "Up, get out of this place, for the Lord will destroy the city." But he appeared to his sons-in-law to be jesting. (v. 14)

Even with impending danger, Lot and his family clung to their city (v. 16). How Lot dragged his feet!

> And it came about when they had brought them outside, that one [angel] said, "Escape for your life! Do not look behind you, and do not stay anywhere in the valley; escape to the mountains, lest you be swept away." But Lot said to them, "Oh no, my lords! Now behold, your servant has found favor in your sight, and you have magnified your lovingkindness, which you have shown me by saving my life; but I cannot escape to the mountains, lest the disaster overtake me and I die; now behold, this town is near enough to flee to, and it is small. Please, let me escape there (is it not small?) that my life may be saved." (vv. 17–20)

And finally, notice how Lot's wife revealed her heart's true home.

> Then the Lord rained on Sodom and Gomorrah brimstone and fire from the Lord out of heaven, and He overthrew those cities, and all the valley, and all the inhabitants of the cities, and what grew on the ground. But his wife, from behind him, looked back; and she became a pillar of salt. (vv. 24–26)

Why would any family hesitate? Why would any wife look back? Why would those carrying out the rescue have to tug and plead as they did? Because Lot's family had deteriorated.

B. Moral compromise (vv. 30–35). A sordid photograph of that family's decline is graphically preserved for us farther down in Genesis 19.

> And Lot went up from Zoar, and stayed in the mountains, and his two daughters with him; for he was

afraid to stay in Zoar; and he stayed in a cave, he and his two daughters. Then the first-born said to the younger, "Our father is old, and there is not a man on earth to come in to us after the manner of the earth. Come, let us make our father drink wine, and let us lie with him, that we may preserve our family through our father." So they made their father drink wine that night, and the first-born went in and lay with her father; and he did not know when she lay down or when she arose. And it came about on the morrow, that the first-born said to the younger, "Behold, I lay last night with my father; let us make him drink wine tonight also; then you go in and lie with him, that we may preserve our family through our father." So they made their father drink wine that night also, and the younger arose and lay with him; and he did not know when she lay down or when she arose. (vv. 30–35)

There are several marks of deterioration that stand out from this passage. First is *an absence of divine perspective.* There is no prayer, no sense of waiting on God, no standard of holiness. Second is *the presence of carnal thoughts.* There is no limit to what a family will do if it lacks moral guidelines. These two young women didn't even flinch as they carried out their incestuous plan. Third is *a breakdown of parental authority.* To these carnal daughters their father seemed like any other man, and they took advantage of his weakness without giving it a second thought. Fourth is *a buildup of sensual toughness.* Their shameless imaginations showed no modesty, no moral restraint, no hesitation. All this represents the silent fallout that accompanies deterioration. Lot is not totally blameless. His passive parenting is reflected in his ignorance of the daughters' intentions. Twice, the passage repeats that "he did not know" that his daughters had done this despicable act (vv. 33, 35).

Do You Know Where Your Children Are?

One of the most important marks of a good parent is being in touch with your children and staying aware of what's going on in their lives.

Remember years ago when the advertisement came on TV: "It's ten o'clock—do you know where your children are?" It made you think, didn't it? It may have even pricked your conscience.

Do you know where your children go? Do you know who they date? Do you know what their dating life is like? Do you talk to them about sex and sensuality? Are you the person they can come to and get their answers—or do they have to get them from the street?

"It's ten o'clock—do you know where your children are?"

There's another kind of not knowing, and that is simply knowing but not taking charge.[4]

Passive Parenting Only Postpones the Pain

Children can forgive parents for just about anything, but the hardest thing for them to forgive is the lack of parental discipline. When they grow up and spend their lives trying to discipline themselves or suffering under some other, harsher authority, they look back on their childhood with resentment. And they wonder, Why didn't my parents help set the boundaries and teach me how to discipline myself?

C. Personal consequences (vv. 36–38). In times of crisis, families that have eroded capsize; they don't stabilize. And personal consequences tip the boat. Notice the ones in Lot's family.

Thus both the daughters of Lot were with child by their father. (v. 36)

Those two acts of incest bore bitter fruit. But lest you think shame accompanied them, look at the names these women gave their father's children.

And the first-born bore a son, and called his name Moab; he is the father of the Moabites to this day. And as for the younger, she also bore a son, and called his name Ben-ammi; he is the father of the sons of Ammon to this day. (vv. 37–38)

Moab literally means "from my father"; Ben-ammi, "son of my people." Even the very names of their sons reflect the daughters' shamelessness. Have you tracked the steps downward that led to this family's deterioration?

—Lot moved his family into a place of extreme debauchery.

—He failed to establish a standard of holiness.

---

4. For example, Eli's relationship to his boys was tragic because he knew their behavior was poor but failed to do anything about it (1 Sam. 2:12–17). David's relationship with Adonijah was no better (1 Kings 1:5–6).

—He became passive in the training of his daughters, content to remain uninformed and uninvolved.

—The daughters ran with men who took spiritual matters lightly.[5]

—When a crisis occurred, no one turned to the Lord.

—Finally, there was incest and a lack of shame.

III. Ways to Guard Against Domestic Erosion

As we have seen, deterioration is not a sudden event. Fortunately, unlike an earthquake, there are warning signs. And if we are attentive to those signs, we can shore up a sagging homelife. Here are four suggestions that can protect your family from dissolving.

A. Realize that no one is immune to domestic erosion. Any life can erode, not just Lot's. It can happen at any age, not just in the teens or mid-life. And it can happen anywhere, not just in Sodom. One thing that will help is to remind yourself: I'm vulnerable . . . it could happen to me . . . there are no guarantees (see 1 Cor. 10:12).

B. Stay alert to subtle hints. Remember, erosion is silent, slow, and insidious. Here are some points to beware of: toleration of the profane, making light of sacred things, lacking embarrassment in shameful situations, poor choice of friends, quiet replacement of biblical standards with the world's standards.

C. Declare and model your standards repeatedly. Why? Because times change and the spiritual edges of our lives get blunted. Because children forget and, as they grow older, they become more clever. They'll test the fences and, if the standard isn't in place, they'll break through and run wild. And remember, children don't demand or require a perfect model—only a consistent, honest one. So if you slip and fall on your face, say so. Don't cover things up to make yourself look good. Admit your failures and ask your children's forgiveness. In doing so, you strengthen their standards.

D. Encourage your children to sustain the same standard as they become adults—when choosing a spouse, a roommate, going off to college, choosing a career and lifestyle. But once they've left the nest, model your values as a continual call to godly living.

5. See lesson titled "When the Cesspool Overflows," p. 79.

🐴 Living Insights

One of the most important marks of good parenting is staying aware of your children's lifestyles and whereabouts. Tragically, some parents are uninformed. Just as sad, some parents know their kids are in trouble yet don't take charge. And some don't even seem to care.

● In our study, we looked at a passive dad, Lot, and the moral breakdown his family experienced as a result of that passivity. Let's do some research and take a closer look at Lot. Check out the Scriptures that tell his story; put yourself in his shoes. Why do you think he behaved as he did? What caused his downfall? How could he have avoided it? Write your conclusions in the space provided.

Lot's Passivity

_____

_____

_____

_____

_____

_____

_____

_____

_____

_____

_____

_____

_____

_____

_____

_____

_____

Continued on next page

Having discussed the deterioration of families, now let's take a look at the qualities of a strong family.

• Six characteristics of a stable family are listed below. Write a brief report on how each is evident in your home—or on how you will begin to build it into your home.

Strong families . . .

—show appreciation toward one another.
—spend time together.
—have good communication.
—are committed to each other.
—have a religious orientation.
—handle crises in a positive manner.

Disobedience Déjà Vu

Genesis 20

Wouldn't it be wonderful if, the moment we accepted Jesus as our personal Savior, everything in our lives could be made whole and right? Experience proves, however, that instantaneous perfection does not happen—it's just not realistic at conversion. Alan Redpath, in *The Making of a Man of God,* reveals this interesting observation:

> The conversion of a soul is the miracle of a moment, the manufacture of a saint is the task of a lifetime.[1]

Even after we have trusted Christ for salvation, we sometimes find ourselves repeating the same sins over and over. Abraham was no exception.

As we reach Genesis 20, Abraham has been away from the city of Haran for twenty-five years. Up to this point, his life has been an adventure of learning experiences. We've seen his greatheartedness, when he gave Lot the first choice of real estate. We've seen his courage, when he rescued Lot from his captors. But we've seen his failures as well, when he mistook Eliezer for the promised child, when he used Hagar as a substitute wife to conceive a son, when he asked Sarah to lie about being his wife. And in our lesson today, we watch him repeat a mistake he made long ago. It's disobedience déjà vu.

I. The Disappointing Reality of Repeated Stanzas

A discordant life grates against God like an off-key song.

A. In biblical days. Abraham wasn't the only biblical figure who sang the same dissonant song more than once.

1. **Moses** (Exod. 2:11–12, Num. 20:8–12). While the Israelites were still captive in Egypt, Moses saw an Egyptian beating a Hebrew slave. In his fury, Moses killed the Egyptian and buried him in the sand. More than forty years later, he found himself frustrated with the Israelites' lack of faith as he led them out of bondage. When God instructed him to strike the rock once to bring forth water, he struck the rock twice instead. We can see from these incidents that Moses had a problem with his temper—and it carried him far beyond God's intent. Because of his inappropriate behavior, God denied him entrance to the Promised Land (v. 12).

2. **The children of Israel** (Exod. 15, 16; Num. 14). The Red Sea deliverance was only three days old when the Israelites began to murmur against God, complaining about the water supply (Exod. 15:22–24). Although God faithfully quenched their thirst with an abundance of clear, sweet water, barely

1. Alan Redpath, *The Making of a Man of God* (Westwood, N.J.: Fleming H. Revell Co., 1962), p. 5.

two weeks later they complained of hunger (16:1–3). Even repeated miracles didn't convince them of God's intention to provide (Num. 14:22–23).

3. **Samson** (Judg. 14, 16). The first recorded words of this Israelite judge are "I saw a woman.... Get her for me, for she looks good to me" (14:2–3). The woman he had seen was a Philistine—an enemy of Israel. When she became Samson's wife, she betrayed him. Twenty years later, his lust lured him into the same mistake ... but this time with fatal results. Delilah's deceit brought about his downfall ... and ultimately his death.

4. **Peter** (Mark 14:27–31, 66–72). The night of His trial, Jesus said that all would forsake Him, but Peter adamantly protested, "Even though all may fall away, yet I will not" (v. 29). Even after Jesus rehearsed Peter's future denials, Peter responded, "Even if I have to die with You, I will not deny You!" (v. 31). That very night Jesus was captured, and as He had said, "all left Him" (vv. 46–50). Three times Peter denied his association with Jesus (vv. 68, 70–71), despite his earlier promises. He repeated the same sin three times ... in the same evening.

B. In our day. Who of us has not complained against the Lord about our circumstances? Who of us has not had to confess sensual lust or lost temper or the denial of our relationship with Christ? Who can claim to have never repeated a mistake? Not one of us can turn up a nose at the errors of Moses, the Israelites, Samson, Peter, or even Abraham ... rather, we should learn from them.

II. Same Song, Second Verse . . . Still Off-Key

Some of us may find Abraham's second-stanza sin comforting, if for no other reason than to realize that those mighty in faith share our weaknesses.

A. Act of disobedience (Gen. 20:1–2). Our story resumes with Abraham on the road again, setting out to make a home in yet another new land.

> Now Abraham journeyed from there toward the land
> of the Negev, and settled between Kadesh and Shur;
> then he sojourned in Gerar. (v. 1)

The record is silent as to why Abraham left the oaks of Mamre and traveled west to Gerar. Perhaps the destruction of the cities in the plain had damaged his pastures, or perhaps personal trauma caused him to pull up stakes. Whatever the case, upon arrival, he sold the inhabitants of Gerar the same bill of goods about Sarah that he had sold to the Eygptians (see 12:11–20).

And Abraham said of Sarah his wife, "She is my sister."
So Abimelech, king of Gerar, sent and took Sarah. (20:2)

B. Consequences of disobedience (vv. 3–7). Abimelech learned the truth about Sarah from God Himself.

But God came to Abimelech in a dream of the night, and said to him, "Behold, you are a dead man because of the woman whom you have taken, for she is married." (v. 3)

Abimelech protested his innocence.

Now Abimelech had not come near her; and he said, "Lord, wilt Thou slay a nation, even though blameless? Did he not himself say to me, 'She is my sister'? And she herself said, 'He is my brother.' In the integrity of my heart and the innocence of my hands I have done this." (vv. 4–5)

God understood, and He gave Abimelech a chance to get out of his sticky situation.

Then God said to him in the dream, "Yes, I know that in the integrity of your heart you have done this, and I also kept you from sinning against Me; therefore I did not let you touch her. Now therefore, restore the man's wife, for he is a prophet, and he will pray for you, and you will live. But if you do not restore her, know that you shall surely die, you and all who are yours." (vv. 6–7)

Abimelech had been innocently drawn into Abraham's deceitfulness. But where sin darkens, grace shines.

C. Grace after disobedience (vv. 7–18). King Abimelech had had a disconcerting night. So he got out of bed early to prepare to confront Abraham (v. 8). And once again, Abraham's sister story—brought out of mothballs to cloak his true identity—was exposed as a sham.

D. Forgiveness and healing (vv. 14–18). God gave good reason why Abimelech should protect Abraham (v. 7). Therefore Abimelech showered gifts upon him: sheep, oxen, servants, and land (vv. 14–15). And then he cleared Sarah's reputation.

And to Sarah he said, "Behold, I have given your brother a thousand pieces of silver; behold, it is your vindication before all who are with you, and before all men you are cleared." (v. 16)

Abraham responded by praying for Abimelech, and forgiveness and healing took place as God had said.

And Abraham prayed to God; and God healed Abimelech and his wife and his maids, so that they bore

children. For the Lord had closed fast all the wombs
of the household of Abimelech because of Sarah,
Abraham's wife. (vv. 17–18)

Our Failures . . . God's Faithfulness

Abraham's tune starts out off-key, but God restores his
melody. Though his lie is not to be excused, the incident
shows us that God does not withdraw His grace because
of our failure. Some of us wince when Abraham is caught
and sigh in relief when he is forgiven a second time, but
we see that God's grace toward Abraham was as sure after
the lie as before it.

Has your song, like Abraham's, become discordant? God
responds to our failures—like Abraham's—with forgiveness. Let His grace restore you to harmony with Him.

III. The Lord's Song Is Harmonious

Three principles will help you sing the Lord's song and keep your
life in tune with godly perspective.

A. Never presume on your weaknesses. Abraham knew it
was dangerous to go back into Egypt. Entering Abimelech's territory just put him in another situation where he would need
to dust off the old sister story to survive. Likewise, if you struggle
with alcohol, is it wise to rent an apartment over a bar? Since
pornography inflames your inner spirit, do you have any business lingering over the magazine counter? Can obesity be solved
in a pastry shop? Can greed be avoided by associating with
greedy people? Of course not. Sin can't be stopped by stepping
on temptation's thin ice.

Baiting the Wolf

Eskimos kill a wolf by exciting the animal's thirst for
fresh blood. Animal blood is applied to a knife blade. The
knife handle is stuck into the snow so that the bloody
blade is pointing up. When a wolf discovers this bait, he
licks it. The taste of fresh blood excites his desire for more,
and he insatiably licks without feeling the razor edge of
the knife cutting his own tongue, as his own blood mingles
with the blood on the knife. His licking frenzy does not
stop—until he drops dead on the snow.[2]

---

2. Paraphrase of Paul Harvey's quote in "Sin's Peril," by Chris T. Zwingelberg, in *Leadership*
(Winter 1987), vol. 8, p. 41.

Are you walking precariously close to snares? Are you drawing your own blood on the sharp knife of sin? If "the call of the wild" has enticed you to fulfill your lusts, it's never too late to tune your ears to the call of the Master and return home to the fireside warmth of His love.

B. Never rely on your own crutches. The walk of faith is to be lived without man-made crutches. Abraham built a crutch when he concocted his sister story and stored it away for future use. Sarah slipped the crutch under his arm when she agreed to go along with the story. She should have said, "Now, dear, supporting you is one thing, but lying for you is another. I won't be a part of your deceitful plans." We often become accomplices to wrong because we are afraid to lovingly confront. In such a situation God calls us not only to throw away our own crutches but also to discourage others from using theirs.

C. Never lean on your own understanding. Abraham summed up his situation and came to the wrong conclusion. We do that too, when we limit our perspectives to the boundaries of human understanding. Proverbs 3:5–6 shows us the advantage of seeking God's wisdom.

Trust in the Lord with all your heart,
And do not lean on your own understanding.
In all your ways acknowledge Him,
And He will make your paths straight.

Living Insights

Study One ▀▀

What we have in Genesis 20 is the same song, second verse—and still off-key! Disobedience is such a terrible pattern in our lives. Let's see if we can profit by examining this chapter more closely.

• Read Genesis 20 and pick out ten key words in the text. Define each term from hints in the verses, then consult a Bible dictionary for a more complete definition. Finally, write a statement about why the word is significant.

Continued on next page

Genesis 20

Key Word _____

Definition _____

_____

Significance _____

_____

Key Word _____

Definition _____

_____

Significance _____

_____

Key Word _____

Definition _____

_____

Significance _____

_____

Key Word _____

Definition _____

_____

Significance _____

_____

Key Word _____

Definition _____

_____

Significance _____

_____

Key Word _____

Definition _____

_____

Significance _____

_____

Key Word _____

Definition _____

_____

Significance _____

_____

Key Word _____

Definition _____

_____

Significance _____

_____

Key Word _____

Definition _____

_____

Significance _____

_____

Key Word _____

Definition _____

_____

Significance _____

_____

Continued on next page

![Living Insights icon] *Living Insights*

What will keep you singing the Lord's song? Trusting Him completely will. Let's talk to the Lord about our lives.

- Once again, our time for Living Insights seems best spent in prayer. Speak to God about breaking the pattern of disobedience in your life. Confess your weaknesses, your crutches, and your self-centeredness to Him. Talk about positive steps you'll be taking to avoid future failures. Ask Him for His strength. Sing His song!

It's a Boy!

Genesis 21:1–7

There are four words we should never forget: *God keeps His word!* He doesn't tell us one thing and then do another. He doesn't lead us on, to let us down. God has veracity—He traffics in truthfulness.

> The faithfulness of God is a datum of sound theology but to the believer it becomes far more than that: it passes through the processes of the understanding and goes on to become nourishing food for the soul. For the Scriptures not only teach truth, they show also its uses for mankind. The inspired writers were men of like passion with us, dwelling in the midst of life. What they learned about God became to them a sword, a shield, a hammer; it became their life motivation, their good hope, and their confident expectation. From the objective facts of theology their hearts made how many thousand joyous deductions and personal applications![1]

I. Two Things to Remember about God's Promises

Learn to lean on God's truthfulness. As you do, you will discover two hallmarks of His promises.

A. God is in no hurry. God does not operate on our timetables. He isn't ruled by wristwatches or appointment books. His promises are timeless . . . and they are fulfilled more by our obedience than by our calendars.

B. God never forgets or retracts His word. If He makes a promise, it will be done. However, a note of caution is in order—not all of the Bible's promises are applicable to all people. Use the following criteria to decide which promises you should take personally.

  1. Is the promise universal in scope? A promise is universal when words like *whoever* or *anyone* are used in Scripture. Romans 10:13 is an example.

> "*Whoever* will call upon the name of the Lord will be saved." (emphasis added)

  Luke 9:23–24 is another universal promise.

> And He was saying to them *all,* "If *anyone* wishes to come after Me, let him deny himself, and take up his cross daily, and follow Me. For *whoever* wishes to save his life shall lose it, but *whoever* loses his life for My sake, he is the one who will save it." (emphasis added)

---

1. A. W. Tozer, *The Knowledge of the Holy* (New York, N.Y.: Harper and Row, Publishers, 1961), p. 86.

Such universal promises are held out to anyone—anytime, anywhere—who will follow their advice.

2. **Is the promise personal in nature?** A specific promise given to someone else is not necessarily meant for you. For example, consider God's word to Paul in Acts 18:9b–10.

> "Do not be afraid any longer, but go on speaking and do not be silent; for I am with you, and no man will attack you in order to harm you, for I have many people in this city."

Genesis 15:13–16 holds another promise with a clearly marked name tag.

> And God said to Abram, "Know for certain that your descendants will be strangers in a land that is not theirs, where they will be enslaved and oppressed four hundred years. But I will also judge the nation whom they will serve; and afterward they will come out with many possessions. And as for you, you shall go to your fathers in peace; you shall be buried at a good old age. Then in the fourth generation they shall return here, for the iniquity of the Amorite is not yet complete."

It's tempting to claim the comfort intended for someone else's ear, but hoping in promises that were never made to you only invites disappointment.

3. **Is the promise conditional?** Some promises are dependent on personal action. That is, if you fulfill the condition, the promise will follow. James 4:10 is one of those promises.

> Humble yourselves in the presence of the Lord, and He will exalt you.

Humbling yourself guarantees personal honor. Consider, too, this familiar promise:

> If we confess our sins, He is faithful and righteous to forgive us our sins and to cleanse us from all unrighteousness. (1 John 1:9)

See how confession of sin secures God's forgiveness (compare Ps. 66:18)? Watch for the conditional aspects within God's promises.

II. God Always Comes Through as He Promised

Early in our study we saw God make a specific promise to Abraham—He said He'd give him a son. It's been twenty-five years since Abraham left Haran (Gen. 12:4), but the time has finally come for that promise to be fulfilled.

A. The Lord provides (Gen. 21:1–2). When things are just right in God's eyes ... when the right moment has come ... He acts. God doesn't forget what He says He'll do.

> Then the Lord took note of Sarah as He had said, and the Lord did for Sarah as He had promised. So Sarah conceived and bore a son to Abraham in his old age, at the appointed time of which God had spoken to him. (vv. 1–2)

Imagine Abraham and Sarah's joy as they cuddle their long-awaited child. They felt ready for him a quarter century ago—but God had other plans. F. B. Meyer comments on their long wait:

> God has His set times. It is not for us to know them; indeed, we cannot know them; we must wait for them. If God had told Abraham in Haran that he must wait for thirty years until he pressed the promised child to his bosom, his heart would have failed him. So, in gracious love, the length of the weary years was hidden, and only as they were nearly spent, and there were only a few more months to wait, God told him that "according to the time of life, Sarah shall have a son" (18:14). ... Take heart, waiting one, thou waitest for One who cannot disappoint thee; and who will not be five minutes behind the appointed moment: ere long "your sorrow shall be turned into joy."[2]

A Time to Give Birth

Is there something or someone you've been waiting for? Has the wait been longer than you expected? Take courage from the new life in Sarah's womb. And remember:

There is an appointed time for everything. And
there is a time for every event under heaven—
A time to give birth, and a time to die;
A time to plant, and a time to uproot what
is planted.
A time to kill, and a time to heal;
A time to tear down, and a time to build up.
A time to weep, and a time to laugh;
A time to mourn, and a time to dance.

---

2. F. B. Meyer, *Abraham; or, The Obedience of Faith* (1968; reprint, Fort Washington, Pa.: Christian Literature Crusade, 1971), p. 119. Evidently, Meyer is not using a strict chronology here. He mentions that Abraham waited thirty years from the time he left Haran to the birth of Isaac, whereas Genesis 12:4 and 21:5 reveal that Abraham actually waited twenty-five years.

> A time to throw stones, and a time to gather
>   stones;
> A time to embrace, and a time to shun
>   embracing.
> A time to search, and a time to give up as
>   lost;
> A time to keep, and a time to throw away.
> A time to tear apart, and a time to sew
>   together;
> A time to be silent, and a time to speak.
> A time to love, and a time to hate;
> A time for war, and a time for peace.
> (Eccles. 3:1–8)
> God didn't miss His appointment with Sarah, and He
> won't miss His appointment with you.

B. Abraham obeys (Gen. 21:3–5). After all the years of waiting, Abraham lost no time in following God's instructions concerning this baby.

> And Abraham called the name of his son who was
> born to him, whom Sarah bore to him, Isaac. (v. 3)

Isaac—the name means "he laughs." Remember ninety-year-old Sarah's reaction to the news that this was the year for the promise to be fulfilled (18:12)? She laughed and was rebuked by God for doing so. But the child's name is more than a reproof. It shouts of the delight this baby brought into the world. Eight days after Isaac's birth, Abraham did to his son what God had earlier required of all the males.

> Then Abraham circumcised his son Isaac when he
> was eight days old, as God had commanded him.
> Now Abraham was one hundred years old when his
> son Isaac was born to him. (21:4–5)

Circumcision is the mark of the Jew; it provides an outward sign for God's people (17:10–12). And indeed Isaac was, from the moment of his conception, a promised son within God's chosen race.

C. Sarah rejoices (21:6–7). It isn't hard to believe that happiness and wonder filled Sarah's heart. Her words in Hebrew have a cadence that sounds like a song.

> "God has made laughter for me; everyone who hears
> will laugh with me.... Who would have said to Abra-
> ham that Sarah would nurse children? Yet I have
> borne him a son in his old age." (vv. 6–7)

There were times when Sarah had given up hope or misinterpreted God's intent (18:11–12). Remember Hagar (chap. 16)? When all human means were exhausted, God did the impossible.[3]

> *"He Giveth More Grace"*
> When we have exhausted our store of
>   endurance,
> When our strength has failed ere the day is half
>   done,
> When we reach the end of our hoarded
>   resources,
> Our Father's full giving is only begun.[4]

III. The Next Time You Have to Wait

If you are in a holding pattern—waiting for God to fulfill His promises—here are four helps to encourage you.

A. Remember, God is not accidentally late. Any delay is divinely appointed. Are you waiting for the fulfillment of a promise? Are you hanging on for dear life, only to have the fingers of your faith pried up one by one, by the enemy? Satan knows how hard it is to wait, and he'll try to convince you that you are forgotten or unimportant. But don't let go! His whisperings are lies—God's word is true (Eph. 6:16).

B. Forget about your own timetable. Your schedule and God's intentions may not mesh, because God does not operate according to your appointment book. Trust His arrangements, and don't panic (1 Pet. 5:6–7).

C. Implore the Lord for new strength and divine wisdom. You will be given needed stability during the difficult times (Isa. 40:31).

D. Ignore the urge to manipulate people. If you don't, you will only transfer your trust from God to others. You will find yourself avoiding the waiting process by manipulating people

---

3. Although the Bible acknowledges the heartbreak of infertility, it does not directly address the solutions current technology offers. So, it is necessary for each Christian to decide regarding the ethical use of such procedures. While not addressing this issue specifically, Lewis B. Smedes, in his book *Mere Morality: What God Expects from Ordinary People* (Grand Rapids, Mich.: William B. Eerdmans Publishing Co., 1983), helps believers develop a personal code of ethics to add wisdom to the decisions they must make in the absence of specific biblical instruction.

4. Annie Johnson Flint, "He Giveth More Grace," © 1941. Renewed 1969 by Lillenas Publishing Co., from *The Hymnal for Worship and Celebration* (Waco, Tex.: Word Music, 1986), no. 415.

to your own ends instead of God's. Trusting God's promises and His timing will give you the kind of assurance you can sleep on (James 3:13–18).

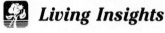

Living Insights

Study One

God keeps His word! He always keeps His promises, but always in His timing. His deliberate delays can teach us many truths and build strong character.

- The birth of Isaac is a great illustration of God's provision following a long wait. The rescue of the enslaved children of Israel after four hundred years is another fine illustration. Can you think of other examples of this concept in Scripture? Try to add to the list other examples that come to mind.

God's Provision in Biblical Times

The birth of Isaac

Delivering the children of Israel from Egypt

_____

_____

_____

_____

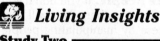

Living Insights

Study Two

It's really helpful to look at examples from the Bible. But it's also beneficial to put God's truth to work in our own experience. Let's personally apply this lesson.

- How has God provided for you personally after one of His deliberate delays? Write down some examples. Then list what you've observed in the lives of those around you. Ask God to show you His provision through this exercise.

God's Provision Today

In my life: _____

_____

_____

_____

_____

_____

_____

_____

_____

_____

In others' lives: _____

_____

_____

_____

_____

_____

_____

_____

_____

_____

Domestic Disharmony

Genesis 21:8–21

God's forgiveness.

It's the Santa Ana winds sweeping brown smog from Southern California skies, restoring them to a clean, virgin blue. It's the spray of the garden hose on a dirty back porch, sending crumpled leaves scudding back to the flower bed. It's a snowplow clearing a path through the blizzard.

It's mercy. Deep. Pure. And wide. Mercy that runs through the dry desert of our sin, quenching our souls where thirst is deserved, cleansing our faces from grime of our own making, soothing our prodigal feet that are sore from running.

God's forgiveness means our souls are forever pure. But though our sins are forgotten, their consequences often live on.

Abraham is a case in point.

I. The Sin-Consequences Syndrome

God's solution to sin's condemnation is personal forgiveness through the finished work of Jesus (Eph. 1:7; Heb. 10:10, 12). A believer who confesses sin is fully forgiven (1 John 1:9). Forgiveness on the vertical plane—between God and man—is guaranteed. However, there is another side of sin that runs horizontally and creates lingering difficulties.

A. A statement to remember. *Though every act of sin is forgivable, the effects of some are not erasable*—their chalk marks show through as a lingering testimony of past mistakes. Such consequences are like tentacles that wrap around and choke relationships.

B. Examples to consider. A person who abuses alcohol or drugs may find God's forgiveness, yet suffer from the effects for a lifetime. The individual who is promiscuous may always be affected by past compromises, experiencing strong emotional repercussions. Profane and cutting words used in times of anger tear and shred like shrapnel, lodging painfully in the heart. Try as you may, these metallic words cannot be surgically removed, ever. And finally, violent acts often result in prison sentences. Murderers may find themselves on their knees ... but on a cold, concrete floor behind a row of steel bars. God is able to forgive the prisoner, who may even be granted a pardon as a result of good behavior, but a prison record follows for a lifetime. Yes, forgiveness may be sought and granted, but the consequences continue.

C. Examples from Scripture. David's affair with Bathsheba started a chain reaction of devastating events (2 Sam. 11–15).

In the same way, Solomon's unbridled lust left his nation reeling (1 Kings 11–12). Samson, blessed with superhuman strength, eventually died because of his sensuality (Judg. 13–16). And Achan caused the defeat of a whole army because of his deceitfulness (Josh. 7:2–5, 19–21).

II. A Specific Case in Point: Abraham and Hagar (Genesis 21:8–21)

Remember Sarah's suggestion that Abraham have a child with Hagar? It's been a long time since she offered that shaky advice, but Ishmael is still around to remind her of it—a lingering consequence.

A. Sarah-Abraham conflict (vv. 8–11). Ishmael has been a sore spot between Abraham and Sarah for fourteen years, but total delight in their son Isaac provides a temporary distraction.

> And the child grew and was weaned, and Abraham made a great feast on the day that Isaac was weaned. (v. 8)

The festive occasion is marred, however, when the older brother challenges the newcomer.

> Now Sarah saw the son of Hagar the Eygptian, whom she had borne to Abraham, mocking. (v. 9)

Ishmael sees Isaac as a rival, and Sarah's new-mother heart rises to the defense of her son.

Sibling Rivalry

Dr. James Dobson observes,

> If American women were asked to indicate *the* most irritating feature of child rearing, I'm convinced that sibling rivalry would get their unanimous vote. Little children (and older ones too) are not content just to hate each other in private. They attack one another like miniature warriors, mobilizing their troops and probing for a weakness in the defensive line. They argue, hit, kick, scream, grab toys, taunt, tattle, and sabotage the opposing forces. . . . The big loser from such combat, of course, is the harassed mother who must listen to the noise of the battlefield and then try to patch up the wounded. If her emotional nature requires peace and tranquillity (and most women do) she may stagger under the barrage of cannonfire.[1]

---

1. James Dobson, *The Strong-Willed Child* (Wheaton, Ill.: Tyndale House Publishers, 1978), pp. 126–27.

By now Sarah has reached the boiling point. Under the pressure of sibling rivalry, she spews her feelings at Abraham.

"Drive out this maid and her son, for the son of this maid shall not be an heir with my son Isaac." (v. 10)

The prejudice in Sarah's words grieves Abraham (v. 11). After all, Ishmael is just as much his son as Isaac. The tensions of the blended family surface, and Ishmael is caught in the middle. It wasn't his decision to join this family. That was someone else's choice, but he is the one who suffers for it. Ishmaels abound even today. The consequences of sin have a ripple effect, touching an ever-widening circle of people caught in its emotional waves.

B. God-Abraham dialogue (vv. 12–13). Abraham is caught in a no-win situation—but God steps in to point the way.

"Do not be distressed because of the lad and your maid; whatever Sarah tells you, listen to her, for through Isaac your descendants shall be named. And of the son of the maid I will make a nation also, because he is your descendant." (vv. 12–13)

God had chosen Isaac, but He hadn't forgotten Ishmael. Strange as it may sound, God had purpose in the sibling rivalry and Sarah's reaction. He knew Ishmael would continue to cause contention in the family and seriously hinder God's purposes for them if he were allowed to remain there (16:12). Sarah was right in driving away Hagar and Ishmael, even though her emotions raged out of control. Though despair fills the account, there is a thread of hope woven into the story. There is a future for Hagar and Ishmael. It's just like God to take tragedy and turn it around for His purposes (21:14–21, Rom. 8:28).

Listen to God's Gift!

A wife is God's gift to her husband (Gen. 2:18). She is to be treated as a treasure—like any valuable gift. Draw on her wisdom and unique perspective. Nurture and facilitate her. You and your family will be blessed.

An excellent wife, who can find?
For her worth is far above jewels.
The heart of her husband trusts in her,
And he will have no lack of gain.
She does him good and not evil
All the days of her life....
Strength and dignity are her clothing,
And she smiles at the future.
She opens her mouth in wisdom,

> And the teaching of kindness is on her
>   tongue....
> Her children rise up and bless her;
> Her husband also, and he praises her, saying:
> "Many daughters have done nobly,
> But you excel them all."
> (Prov. 31:10–12, 25–26, 28–29)

C. God-Hagar encounter (Gen. 21:14–21). Abraham's heart must have been breaking as he carried out God's instruction. But there is no hesitation on his part.

> So Abraham rose early in the morning, and took bread and a skin of water, and gave them to Hagar, putting them on her shoulder, and gave her the boy, and sent her away. And she departed, and wandered about in the wilderness of Beersheba. (v. 14)

Once again, Hagar is in the wilderness with her child (see 16:6–7). But this time, as her supplies are exhausted, she doesn't panic but turns to God.

> And the water in the skin was used up, and she left the boy under one of the bushes. Then she went and sat down opposite him, about a bowshot away, for she said, "Do not let me see the boy die." And she sat opposite him, and lifted up her voice and wept. (21:15–16)

If a cameraman were following these events, he would capture a close-up of the trauma of separation and then pan out across a barren wilderness. We would watch as Hagar and Ishmael are assaulted by the hot sun until their resources are depleted and their walk turns to stumbling, thirst, and hunger. Finally, we'd see Ishmael collapse and Hagar cry out to God, "Do not let me see the boy die." All she can do is lift up her voice and weep. The pathos of this scene is worth considering. Hagar left without any security except food, water, and a promise from God (16:10). She faced a veritable wasteland. Those of you who are being emotionally or physically abused and continue in the relationship because you are afraid of the financial, emotional, and physical wilderness, pay attention to Hagar's situation.[2] Even though she suffered greatly, her need for support was supplied.

> And God heard the lad crying; and the angel of God called to Hagar from heaven, and said to her, "What

---

2. If you are in an abusive relationship, please read James Dobson's *Love Must Be Tough: New Hope for Families in Crisis* (Waco, Tex.: Word Books, 1983).

is the matter with you, Hagar? Do not fear, for God
has heard the voice of the lad where he is. Arise, lift
up the lad, and hold him by the hand; for I will make
a great nation of him." Then God opened her eyes and
she saw a well of water; and she went and filled the
skin with water, and gave the lad a drink. (vv. 17–19)
The boy grew, learned the ways of the desert, and became an
archer (v. 20). Hagar and her son survived—apart from Abraham's resources! Hagar even presented Ishmael with an Egyptian
wife (v. 21). God did not forget Hagar. Nor did He forget His
promise to greatly multiply her descendants (16:10). God had
compassion on Hagar's plight and became like a father to
Ishmael. A beautiful example of Psalm 68:5–6.

A father of the fatherless and a judge for the widows,
Is God in His holy habitation.
God makes a home for the lonely;
He leads out the prisoners into prosperity,
Only the rebellious dwell in a parched land.

And consequently, God became like a husband to the abandoned
Hagar. A perfect illustration of Isaiah 54:5.

"For your husband is your Maker,
Whose name is the Lord of hosts;
And your Redeemer is the Holy One of Israel,
Who is called the God of all the earth."

III. Sin's Consequences and Lessons to Be Learned
Harsh domestic problems offer excellent built-in lessons for living.

**A. Sinful consequences will disturb, but they need not
defeat us.** God's purposes are much broader than our failures.
There is hope for all who lean on Him during the difficult times
(Gen. 50:15–21).

**B. Marital conflicts will disrupt, but they need not com-
pletely destroy us.** Godly people have marital disagreements
and failures, but defensiveness and accusation only sidestep the
path to solutions. Better to listen and learn than to lash back
(Eph. 4:29–32).

**C. Personal confusion will disarm, but it needn't com-
pletely demoralize us.** Being God's child guarantees a future and a hope (Heb. 10:35–36, 12:3–11).

🌹 *Living Insights*

Talk about domestic disharmony! Abraham was up to his ears in trouble with Sarah, Hagar, and Ishmael. Let's look at the tension in these relationships.

• Following is a list of the relationships in this account. Reread the passage and summarize what it says concerning them. If the passage is silent, conjecture what it might have been like.

Abraham and Sarah _____

_____

_____

Abraham and Hagar _____

_____

_____

Abraham and Ishmael _____

_____

_____

Sarah and Hagar _____

_____

_____

Sarah and Ishmael _____

_____

_____

Hagar and Ishmael _____

_____

_____

Continued on next page

Living Insights

For those of us who are married, a study such as this one can bring a renewed appreciation for our mates. When was the last time you expressed that appreciation? Why not show it this week? Today?

- How does your mate most like to be shown appreciation? Take some time to express just how much you care. Be thoughtful, sensitive, and honest. Whether it's a note, a date, or a small gift, make sure your appreciation shines through!

A Well, a Tree, and a Covenant

Genesis 21:22–34

As a way of restoring order to a maddening family pace, parents often tell their children to stop, sit down, and be quiet. Adults, like children, also get caught up in a frantic lifestyle and have equal difficulty taking time out to settle down and be quiet.

> This is the age
> Of the half-read page.
> And the quick hash
> And the mad dash.
> The bright night
> With the nerves tight.
> The plane hop
> And the brief stop.
> The lamp tan
> In a short span.
> The Big Shot
> In a good spot.
> And the brain strain
> And the heart pain.
> And the cat naps
> Till the spring snaps—
> And the fun's done![1]

It's easy to get caught up in "the mad dash." But to stop and honestly evaluate our lives is an enormous challenge—a challenge Abraham decisively confronted.

Abraham knew when it was time to pull away from the crowd and rest, and he had a special place for doing that. As we shall see in this lesson, his example is one well worth emulating.

I. Essential Interludes of Personal Preparation

Personal survival in a fast-paced society is, let's face it, difficult. We rarely give ourselves permission to enjoy an interlude of quietness. A frenzied pace, frayed nerves, and general shallowness are, sadly, the rule rather than the exception. Life lived in a hurry makes us superficial, fragile, and spiritually depleted. So when the real tests come, we're unprepared for them.

---

1. Virginia Brasier, "Time of the Mad Atom," as quoted in *Of Quarks, Quasars, and Other Quirks: Quizzical Poems for the Supersonic Age,* collected by Sara Brewton, John E. Brewton, and John Brewton Blackburn (New York, N.Y.: Thomas Y. Crowell Co., 1977), p. 2. Reprinted with permission of the Saturday Evening Post. © 1949 The Curtis Publishing Company.

A. Our need to take time and be still. In the rush of daily living, we begin to settle for less than God's best. We fail to deepen our thoughts and thereby become people who react, rather than order our lives. Gordon MacDonald, in *Ordering Your Private World,* lists eight characteristics of "driven" people.[2]

1. A driven person is most often gratified only by accomplishment.
2. A driven person is preoccupied with the symbols of accomplishment.
3. A driven person is usually caught in the uncontrolled pursuit of expansion.
4. Driven people tend to have a limited regard for integrity.
5. Driven people often possess limited or undeveloped people skills.
6. Driven people tend to be highly competitive.
7. A driven person often possesses a volcanic force of anger, which can erupt any time he senses opposition or disloyalty.
8. Driven people are usually abnormally busy.

Burnout versus Rust-Out?

A popular phrase among some busy Christians is "I'd rather burn out than rust out!" It sounds good—self-sacrificing and spiritual. But whichever way you go, you end up in the same place—out.

God isn't interested in depleting our physical strength or sapping our emotions or neglecting our relationships for the sake of the gospel. Far from it! In fact, the sight of His children rushing from one meeting to another, seldom taking time to nourish their souls with quiet and rest and play, distresses Him (Matt. 11:28–30).

According to an old Greek maxim, you will break the bow if you keep it always bent. Check your bowstring. Is it too tight? Maybe it's time to relax the tension—to sit down and sharpen your personal arrows.

B. Some examples. Being driven isn't just a modern-day problem. Plenty of biblical characters suffered from it as well.

   1. Moses. As Israel's leader, Moses crammed his schedule with meetings from morning to night in order to judge his people's problems (Exod. 18:13). Jethro, his father-in-law,

---

2. Gordon MacDonald, *Ordering Your Private World* (Nashville, Tenn.: Thomas Nelson Publishers, Oliver-Nelson, 1985), pp. 31–36.

saw Moses' predicament and urged him to slow down and delegate his work.

> "You will surely wear out, both yourself and these people who are with you, for the task is too heavy for you; you cannot do it alone." (v. 18)

2. **David.** In exile and fighting battle after battle—not only on the field but in his conscience—David had little energy left to face the crises confronting him. Dismissed from his post, he arrived home to find his village burned, the women and children captured, and his men turned against him. As pressure mounted, he turned to God (1 Sam. 30:1–6).

3. **Martha.** Martha was so concerned with her dinner preparations that she almost missed the whole purpose of her party—to listen to Jesus (Luke 10:38–42).

4. **The disciples.** When the disciples were too busy with the ministry to even eat, Jesus deliberately pulled them aside for a rest (Mark 6:31).

II. Abraham's Days of Quietness and Peace

In Genesis 21, we find Abraham taking a much-needed break. The recent birth of Isaac and the turmoil related to Hagar and Ishmael have taken their toll, and it's time for Abraham to pull aside and be refreshed. And, though he doesn't realize it, his rest is preparing him for the greatest test of his life.

A. Refreshment from the well (vv. 22–32). Apparently, at some point, Abraham's men had dug a well. It became a source of refreshment in that parched land; but, as our story begins, Abimelech's men have seized it.

Guard Your Source of Rest

All of us need our wells of refreshment—places where we can retreat from life's demands to rest and rebuild. But sometimes those times and places will be invaded or taken over by others. And when they are, we need to retrieve them as Abraham did.

So Abraham confronts Abimelech.

> Abraham complained to Abimelech because of the well of water which the servants of Abimelech had seized. (v. 25)

But Abimelech pleads innocence.

> "I do not know who has done this thing; neither did you tell me, nor did I hear of it until today." (v. 26)

The well is important enough to Abraham that he initiates a covenant with Abimelech to guarantee his future access to it.

And Abraham took sheep and oxen, and gave them
to Abimelech; and the two of them made a covenant.
Then Abraham set seven ewe lambs of the flock by
themselves. And Abimelech said to Abraham, "What
do these seven ewe lambs mean, which you have set
by themselves?" And he said, "You shall take these
seven ewe lambs from my hand in order that it may
be a witness to me, that I dug this well." (vv. 27–30)

F. B. Meyer comments on the significance of the seven lambs:

Writing materials were not then in use; but the seven
ewe lambs . . . were the visible and lasting memorial
that the well was his recognized property.[3]

Abraham named the watering place Beersheba, or "the well of
seven" as evidence of the transaction.

Therefore he called that place Beersheba; because
there the two of them took an oath. (v. 31)

B. Enjoyment from the tree (v. 33). Now that the well is his
again, Abraham plants a tamarisk tree beside it. Beneath the
branches he can enjoy cool water and sanctuary from the sear-
ing Negev sun. In the shade of that tree, Abraham "called on the
name of the Lord, the Everlasting God," just as he had in the
cool shade of Moreh's oaks (12:6–8). Away from the demands
of his family and home, he has time to focus on God.

The Names of God

The names Abraham ascribes to God reflect facets of
His character. For example, after he rescued Lot from cap-
tivity, he referred to God as *El Elyon,* or "God Most High"
(14:1–17, 22). In another encounter, he spoke of God as *El
Shaddai,* or "God Almighty" (17:1). In our passage today,
Abraham calls Him "Everlasting God" (21:33).[4]

The Old Testament is replete with the names God's
people used to describe Him. How well acquainted are you
with His character? What names could you give Him to
represent His involvement at critical junctures in your life?

C. Security in the covenant (vv. 32, 34). Abimelech and his
military commander accept Abraham's terms for peace.

So they made a covenant at Beersheba; and Abimelech and Phicol, the commander of his army, arose

---

3. F. B. Meyer, *Abraham; or, The Obedience of Faith* (1968; reprint, Fort Washington, Pa.:
Christian Literature Crusade, 1971), p. 125.

4. *El Olam* is the Hebrew equivalent of "Everlasting God."

and returned to the land of the Philistines. . . . And Abraham sojourned in the land of the Philistines for many days.

Later, in Genesis 22, Abraham will face a dramatic test of his faith when God asks him to sacrifice Isaac. But to equip Abraham for that test, God gives him a pleasant interlude of harmony and tranquility.

III. Seldom-Mentioned Thoughts on Being Still

Concerning the subject of being still, Psalm 46:10 holds an important exhortation: " 'Cease striving and know that I am God.' " We are to cease—desist, back off, let go! And this admonition is given in the context not of a backyard hammock but of a battlefield. Let's find out how we can step aside and gain fresh perspective in the midst of all the little wars raging around our busy lives.

A. Being still calls for a place where we can order our private worlds. Private times with the Lord yield *simplicity*. As we spend time with God, our lives gain security and balance. Consequently, our need to cling to others diminishes.

B. Being still gives us time in which we can rethink our public worlds. And that results in *harmony*. Some of us ricochet through peoples' lives, leaving them offended, confused, and frustrated. Time alone with God tempers our spirits with peaceableness.

C. Being still provides us an opportunity to see ourselves as we really are. Time alone gives us a chance to face *reality*. When we do that, we discover our weaknesses and strengths, and why we succeed at some things and fail at others.

D. Being still allows us the privilege of knowing God as He really is. Knowing God brings us *stability*. God enjoys revealing Himself to those who seek Him, and He invites us to trust Him. As we do, we discover Him to be an unfailing refuge.

> ### A Closing Thought
> In every life
> There's a pause that is better than onward rush,
> Better than hewing or mightiest doing;
> 'Tis the standing still at Sovereign will.
>
> There's a hush that is better than ardent
>   speech,
> Better than sighing or wilderness crying;
> 'Tis the being still at Sovereign will.

The pause and the hush sing a double song
In unison low and for all time long.
O human soul, God's working plan
Goes on, nor needs the aid of man!
Stand still, and see!
Be still, and know![5]

 Living Insights

Study One

It's easy to breeze right through this chapter without realizing all that is there for us in between the lines. Just like Abraham, let's pursue an interlude of quietness and peace.

- Use your Living Insights today as a time of unhurried, meditative reading through some of your favorite psalms. If you don't know where to begin, try Psalm 46. Allow the Lord to cultivate stillness in your life.

 Living Insights

Study Two

All of us need wells of refreshment. We benefit by taking time to retreat, rest, and rebuild. If we're not careful, however, someone or something may interrupt those times.

- Make a plan for consistent interludes of quiet. It may be scheduling a regular walk in the woods or a long drive or a jog in the park. Do whatever best relaxes and refreshes you. But remember, things will come up that try to steal your time away. So make a commitment to protect it!

5. V. Raymond Edman, *The Disciplines of Life* (Minneapolis, Minn.: World Wide Publications, 1948), p. 83.

When God Says, "Let Go!"

Genesis 22:1–14

Our daily lives are built around people and things we enjoy: special friends, a spouse, a business venture, possessions, future plans. These are the pillars and beams of our earthly support system—and if one of them is removed, we sometimes feel as though the framework of our lives is collapsing around us. But there are times when God says, "Let go!" and the nuts and bolts that hold our world together suddenly snap. If you've ever been in that situation, you know the pressure a test like that can exert on your faith.

Abraham, too, was well acquainted with such strenuous tests. In today's lesson, we'll take a look at one that challenged his confidence in God, and we'll see how his unwavering example encourages us to steady our own lives in times of testing.

I. Categories to Be Held Loosely

No matter what or who we lose, letting go is a painful process.

A. Possessions. With the suddenness of lightning, fire rages through a home ... tidal waves flood coastline condominiums ... tornadoes level a town. And a lifetime of possessions can be turned to ash ... mud ... rubble.

B. Businesses, occupations, and projects. Business reversals, loss of employment, failure of pet projects ... these can obliterate a lifetime of work and investment.

C. Plans and dreams. Goals fail and ideas fizzle. We all have personal dreams ... of getting that degree, making that business investment, starting that ministry, having that marriage. But some of those plans are never realized, and the death of these aspirations can be excruciating.

D. People and relationships. There is probably nothing more difficult than losing a loved one. Have you ever stood beside a grave and struggled to let go? And who can possibly describe the feelings of rejection and loneliness initiated by divorce? Grown children struggle with leaving their parents, and parents have difficulty letting their children pursue their own lives. Employers suffer when valued employees leave. And we've all experienced difficult good-byes at an airport terminal or beside a loaded moving van.

II. When God Told Abraham, "Let Go!"

Sometimes people and things can become too important to us. We grip them with closed fists and white knuckles, and God has to pry open our fingers to loosen our hold. Perhaps that's how it was between Abraham and Isaac.

A. God's command (Gen. 22:1–2). Abraham has experienced many tests by the time chapter 22 opens, but none of them compare to what he is about to face.[1]

> Now it came about after these things, that God tested Abraham, and said to him, "Abraham!" And he said, "Here I am." And He said, "Take now your son, your only son, whom you love, Isaac, and go to the land of Moriah; and offer him there as a burnt offering on one of the mountains of which I will tell you." (vv. 1–2)

God's command is clear. This is to be Abraham's greatest test. Aren't there times when your future seems to balance on a single decision? Abraham is at that point. Does he do what God asks, or does he ignore Him as though He has never spoken? Notice when God tests him—after his heart has become affectionately entwined with his son.

> Nothing else in the circumference of his [Abraham's] life could have been such a test as anything connected with the heir of promise, the child of his old age, the laughter of his life.... So He put him to a supreme test, that all men might henceforth know that a mortal man could love God so much as to put Him first, though his dearest lay in the opposite scale of the balance of the heart.[2]

God did not require the boy to serve in the temple as Samuel had, rather He called for Isaac's very life—as a burnt offering—all, or nothing.[3] God wants to test the authenticity of Abraham's faith, and his teenage son is His best tool.

"Lord, I'm Yours"

There are times when we look up full-hearted and prayerfully say, "O, Lord, in this crisp, clear, beautiful moment, You have everything that I own. You have all of me. There is nothing, nothing that I hold back."

---

1. The Hebrew verb translated "tested" is in the piel stem, and that conveys intensity. Music's equivalent is the *fortissimo.* It always conveys passion. This verse could be rendered, "God *severely* tested Abraham" or "God *passionately* tested Abraham."

2. F. B. Meyer, *Abraham; or, The Obedience of Faith* (1968; reprint, Fort Washington, Pa.: Christian Literature Crusade, 1971), p. 131.

3. The burnt offering, *olah,* is derived from the root *alah,* meaning "to go up," as in smoke. See Robert Baker Girdlestone's *Synonyms of the Old Testament* (Grand Rapids, Mich.: William B. Eerdmans Publishing Co., reproduction of the second edition, which appeared in 1897), pp. 187–89. The burnt offering was voluntary, and all of the victim was consumed (Lev. 1:2–9).

It's amazing how soon after those times of commitment God seems to require something sacred in our lives that puts us to the test.

The next time God claims what charms you most, return here... to this story of one who experienced that anguish as well.

B. Abraham's obedience (vv. 3–10). Abraham chooses to obey God's command. There are three wonderful things about his obedience.

   1. **It was immediate** (vv. 3–4). We read of no plea bargaining, rationalizing, arguing, resisting, or doubting. Abraham hears and instantly obeys.

      So Abraham rose early in the morning and saddled his donkey, and took two of his young men with him and Isaac his son; and he split wood for the burnt offering, and arose and went to the place of which God had told him. On the third day Abraham raised his eyes and saw the place from a distance. (vv. 3–4)

      Imagine how Abraham must have felt as he saw the outline of Moriah on the horizon and was about to look at his only son for the last time.

   2. **It was based on faith** (vv. 5–8). Abraham resolves to do as the Lord directed.

      And Abraham said to his young men, "Stay here with the donkey, and I and the lad *will go* yonder; and we *will worship* and *return* to you." (v. 5, emphasis added)

      How can Abraham be so confident that he and Isaac will not only go and worship, but also *return?* Isn't Isaac to be sacrificed? We find the answer in the book of Hebrews.

      By faith Abraham, when he was tested, offered up Isaac; and he who had received the promises was offering up his only begotten son; it was he to whom it was said, "In Isaac your descendants shall be called." He considered that God is able to raise men even from the dead; from which he also received him back as a type. (Heb. 11:17–19)

      Abraham had been promised descendants through Isaac. And if he had learned anything, it was that God keeps His word! So, Abraham reasons, if Isaac is to be slain, God must be planning to raise him from the dead. In the midst of this incredible test, his faith never wavers (compare Rom. 4:20–21).

> And Abraham took the wood of the burnt offering
> and laid it on Isaac his son, and he took in his
> hand the fire and the knife. So the two of them
> walked on together. (Gen. 22:6)

Abraham knows what is coming. Isaac, however, doesn't,
and he innocently inquires:

> "Behold, the fire and the wood, but where is the
> lamb for the burnt offering?" (v. 7b)

To which his father responds:

> "God will provide for Himself the lamb for the
> burnt offering, my son." (v. 8a)

We see no hint that Abraham is bitter toward God—no signs
of argument or doubt. On the contrary, every step up the
mountain is taken in trust.

3. **It was thorough and complete** (vv. 9–10). With methodical
movement, with silent obedience, Abraham prepares for the
sacrifice.

> Then they came to the place of which God had
> told him; and Abraham built the altar there, and
> arranged the wood, and bound his son Isaac, and
> laid him on the altar on top of the wood. And
> Abraham stretched out his hand, and took the
> knife to slay his son. (vv. 9–10)

Isaac's spirit is as strong as his father's; nowhere is there
record that Isaac struggled against his father. He, too, trusted
and obeyed. This is a profound tribute to a strong father-son
relationship.

Fathers, Sons, and Courage

George Jaeger took his father and three sons out
to the Atlantic Ocean to fish. But before day's end,
he would see each of his sons and his father die of
exhaustion.

The boat's engine had stalled in the late
afternoon. While increasing winds whipped
the sea into great waves, the boat rolled
helpless in the water and then began to list
dangerously. When it became apparent that
they were sinking, the five Jaeger men put
on the life vests, tied themselves together ...
and slipped into the water. ...

Six-foot waves and a strong current made
the swimming almost impossible. First one
boy, and then another—and another ...

---

swallowed too much water. Helpless,
George Jaeger watched [each one of] his
sons and then his father die. Eight hours
later, he staggered onto the shore, still pulling the rope that bound the bodies of the
other four to him.

"I realized they were all dead—my three
boys and my father—but I guess I didn't
want to accept it, so I kept swimming all
night long," he said to reporters. "My
youngest boy, Clifford, was the first to go.
*I had always taught our children not to fear
death* because it was being with Jesus
Christ. Before he died I heard him say, 'I'd
rather be with Jesus than go on fighting.' "

Performance under stress is one test of
effective leadership. It may also be the
proof of accomplishment when it comes to
evaluating the quality of a father.... The
beautiful way they died said something
about the kind of father George Jaeger had
been for fifteen years.[4]

Fathers, are you effectively planting seeds of courage in the hearts of your sons and daughters? You are
a model before your children, and they are a mirror
of your courage. Observe their responses in a crisis.
Do you see yourself in the reflection?

C. Heaven's reward (vv. 11–14). Abraham's arm is extended upward over his son, knife poised, ready to plunge. But the action
is arrested by an urgent voice.

But the angel of the Lord called to him from heaven,
and said, "Abraham, Abraham!" And he said, "Here I
am." And he said, "Do not stretch out your hand
against the lad, and do nothing to him; for now I
know that you fear God, since you have not withheld
your son, your only son, from Me." (vv. 11–12)

God knew what Abraham would do. It was Abraham who needed
to see the extent of his own faith.

Then Abraham raised his eyes and looked, and behold, behind him a ram caught in the thicket by his

4. Gordon MacDonald, *The Effective Father* (Wheaton, Ill.: Tyndale House Publishers, 1981),
pp. 13–14.

horns; and Abraham went and took the ram, and offered him up for a burnt offering in the place of his son. And Abraham called the name of that place The Lord Will Provide, as it is said to this day, "In the mount of the Lord it will be provided." (vv. 13–14)

III. When God Tells You, "Let Go!"

This story isn't merely ancient history. It's a lesson for today.

A. **What you *retain* for yourself is usually what God asks you to release to Him.** If you are holding onto something too tightly, *release* your grip and watch God work. If something or someone has become more important to you than it should, God is likely to address your possessiveness.

B. **What you *release* to God, He *replaces* with something even more valuable.** In Abraham's case, God requested and returned Isaac. Having gone through the testing, Abraham was able to value his son with new objectivity. Though Isaac was his son, he belonged to God for His purposes. Abraham understood and released his grip on Isaac only to receive him back again with deeper appreciation for his son . . . and God's ways. Whatever you release to God will increase your value of God's purposes.

C. **When God *replaces*, He also *rewards*** (vv. 15–17). What began as great loss for Abraham became his greatest gain. God rewards obedience.

A Private Prayer

"Father, I want to know Thee, but my coward heart fears to give up its toys. I cannot part with them without inward bleeding, and I do not try to hide from Thee the terror of the parting. I come trembling, but I do come. Please root from my heart all those things which I have cherished so long and which have become a very part of my living self, so that Thou mayest enter and dwell there without a rival. Then shalt Thou make the place of Thy feet glorious. Then shall my heart have no need of the sun to shine in it, for Thyself wilt be the light of it, and there shall be no night there. In Jesus' Name, Amen."[5]

---

5. A. W. Tozer, *The Pursuit of God* (Wheaton, Ill.: Tyndale House Publishers, n.d.), p. 31.

Living Insights

What parent can read this account and not be stirred? This passage rivets our attention through to the very end. It's the kind of story that makes you stop and ask, "What if God put *me* to that test?"

• Write your own version of Genesis 22:1–14. Delve into the emotions Abraham, Isaac, and even Sarah must have experienced. Put yourself in their shoes. Then take the story a little farther. What would the journey home have been like? How would Sarah have greeted Abraham and Isaac?

_____

_____

_____

_____

_____

_____

_____

_____

_____

_____

_____

_____

_____

_____

_____

_____

_____

Continued on next page

🐾 *Living Insights*

Most of us, after reading about Abraham and Isaac, just want to put our arms around our children and hug them close. This story does more than highlight Abraham's faith . . . it also upholds the value of our children.

- Do something special to communicate your appreciation to your children. A few lessons ago you did this for your mate; now turn your focus toward your children. Try writing them a letter. In it, concentrate on statements of love, encouragement, and affirmation. Since many parents don't do this sort of thing often, your letter could become one of the most valuable possessions your children have.

The Pleasures of
Passing God's Exams
Genesis 22:11–19

Have you ever sensed a dumpish atmosphere among your Christian brothers and sisters? This downer attitude is not spoken as much as it is felt. The "woe is me" attitude often drowns out the excitement of life. Instead of "you tell me your dream, and I'll tell you mine," it's "you cry on my shoulder, and I'll cry on yours." Instead of seeing life as a challenge, too often we see it as a burden, like a heavy hand drawing rutted lines of discouragement across our faces. Should our adventure with Christ call us to perpetual gloom? Or should His joy shine in our lives even when trials gather in clouds above us?

I. A Sad Song Sung Often and Played in a Minor Key
Thunderclouds pass over each of our lives. But some of us dwell on the storm rather than the brilliant blue sky that follows. As a result, the robin's song is diminished by our tears. When we focus on the dark side of life, the temptation is to let its sadness dominate us. For some of us, pessimism is a way of life, a shadow that stalks every step we take . . . every thought we think. We dwell on failing marriages instead of healthy ones. Too readily, we point out church leaders who fall and churches that split, instead of praising faithful pastors and flocks. But difficulties don't have to get us down. The book of Proverbs gives us a lesson in optimism. Solomon never glossed over the chuckholes in the road, but he didn't get stuck in them, either. Let's look at some examples of his perspective.

The backslider in heart will have his fill of his own ways,
But a good man will be satisfied with his.
(Prov. 14:14)
Sure, a few of us backslide. But many do not because they are satisfied with life. Here's more good news:
All the days of the afflicted are bad,
But a cheerful heart has a continual feast.
(15:15)
And more:
The Lord is far from the wicked,
But He hears the prayer of the righteous.
Bright eyes gladden the heart;
Good news puts fat on the bones.
(vv. 29–30)
Hard times hit all of us. But our hearts needn't starve. They can stay filled and healthy by feasting on the good news in Scripture.

131

All this brings us back to Abraham, on the heels of the most significant test of his life. Abraham was commanded to offer his son as a sacrifice on the slopes of Mount Moriah, and he never once complained. A beautiful example of optimism, he was convinced that his story would have a happy ending. He knew not only that God brings tests but that, when passed, they pave the way for good things to come into our lives.

II. Joyful Principles of Obedience to Remember

Flash back to Genesis 22:10 where Abraham is obediently bent over his son, his arm extended upward, knife in hand. God stepped into that scene in four ways, just as He does for us when we are obedient.

A. When we obey, God becomes more real (v. 11).

> But the angel of the Lord called to him from heaven, and said, "Abraham, Abraham!" And he said, "Here I am."

At this epochal moment, Abraham and his heavenly Father became inseparably connected. There is nothing like an intense test to draw us closer to our Lord, to make us feel one with Him.

B. When we obey, God relieves the pressure as He affirms our faith. God is not out to destroy us. His tests are designed to show us the strength of our own faith. And between the tests He sends parentheses of pleasure and relief.

> And he said, "Do not stretch out your hand against the lad, and do nothing to him; for now I know that you fear God, since you have not withheld your son, your only son, from Me." (v. 12)

Handling Pressure

Abraham must have felt tremendous pressure when he placed his son on that altar. Have you ever felt that if one more problem were placed on your shoulders you would collapse under the weight?

God isn't interested in producing driven, frenzied people, etching out a pressure cooker living. He's interested in producing people of faith and obedience.

But life has another agenda. It tyrannizes us with a steady badgering of urgent things. Not important things,

---

necessarily. Only urgent. Responsibilities that must be done, and done now. Much of the time, they are good pursuits. But remember that good is often the enemy of the best. And if good activities are robbing you of quiet time with God, they're keeping you from the best.

Though a storm of circumstances whips around you in tyrannizing torrents, remember the verse: " 'Cease striving and know that I am God' " (Ps. 46:10a). If you can do that, you will experience a calm much like the tranquility that follows a thunderstorm.

C. When we obey, God provides. He meets needs in surprising ways. Abraham untied Isaac and watched him climb down from the altar. As he did, God met his need in a wonderful way.

> Then Abraham raised his eyes and looked, and behold, behind him a ram caught in the thicket by his horns; and Abraham went and took the ram, and offered him up for a burnt offering in the place of his son. And Abraham called the name of that place The Lord Will Provide, as it is said to this day, "In the mount of the Lord it will be provided." (Gen. 22:13–14)

On Mount Moriah, Abraham came to a critical point in his relationship with God. At that crossroad, obedience and disobedience intersected on perpendicular paths. If he would have disobeyed God, his life would have taken a hard turn to the left and negatively affected generations to come. But he chose rather to obey; as a result, God greatly blessed him and his descendants.

Insight at the Intersection

We spend a lot of time on life's highway. And every once in a while we come to a crossroad—a place where a decision needs to be made. Slow down when you come to one. Sometimes there are lights. Sometimes there is traffic. But there is always danger. Many people lose the edge of their Christian vitality because they speed right through the crossroad or make an unwise decision at that point.

So when you come to a crossroad in your life, STOP . . . LOOK . . . LISTEN . . . and, most of all, OBEY.

D. When we obey, God multiplies His blessings as He ratifies His promises. Two times the angel of the Lord magnified Abraham's obedience.

> Then the angel of the Lord called to Abraham a second time from heaven, and said, "By Myself I have sworn, declares the Lord, *because you have done this thing, and have not withheld your son,* your only son, indeed I will greatly bless you, and I will greatly multiply your seed as the stars of the heavens, and as the sand which is on the seashore; and your seed shall possess the gate of their enemies. And in your seed all the nations of the earth shall be blessed, *because you have obeyed My voice."* (vv. 15–18, emphasis added)

And blessings flowed, not only to the nation of Israel, but to the whole world as well (Gal. 3:8–9).

III. Next Time You're Tempted to Major in the Minors

In our day, many prophets of doom major in the minor keys by pointing out the negatives. Next time you are invited to join in a chorus of the doldrums, remember three simple suggestions.

A. Reflect on the benefits that have come your way. It's easy to forget the blessings of God, especially when little value is attached to them. Let Psalm 103 heighten the importance of God's gifts.

> Bless the Lord, O my soul,
> And forget none of His benefits;
> Who pardons all your iniquities;
> Who heals all your diseases;
> Who redeems your life from the pit;
> Who crowns you with lovingkindness and
>   compassion;
> Who satisfies your years with good things,
> So that your youth is renewed like the eagle. (vv. 2–5)

Savor the verbs: *pardons, heals, redeems, crowns, satisfies,* and *renews*—all benefits from God.

B. Refuse to allow the few negatives to eclipse the many positives. Introduce thankfulness into thoughts and conversations that are starting to slide toward self-pity or bitterness. Instead of dwelling on the negatives, focus on the positive things God is doing in your life—in your marriage, your home, your job, your school, your church. It's amazing how a few positive words can open a window to God's sunshine and fresh air and give your circumstances a whole new look.

C. Renew your motivation by decreasing your expectations. Rather than set yourself up for a siege of depression, moderate your expectations. The honeymoon is a perfect example. If you build it up to be a cloud nine utopia, you may be setting yourself up for major disappointment by over-anticipation. But if you come down to reality and decrease your expectations, the honeymoon, and all of life for that matter, will more likely be full of surprises and delight.

 Living Insights

Study One ━━━━━━━━━━━━━━━━━━━━━━━━━━━━━━━━━━━━

Genesis 22 is not the sort of chapter one wants to hurry through. It's well worth the time and energy to review the wonderful lessons we've learned in this passage from God's book of jewels.

- Locate a different version of the Scriptures than you usually use and reread the eight rubies in Genesis 22. Input from another translation or paraphrase may provide additional insight into this valuable text.

 Living Insights

Study Two ━━━━━━━━━━━━━━━━━━━━━━━━━━━━━━━━━━━━

Some view life as a challenge, while others view it as a burden. How do you view it? Do you rejoice in the blessings of life, or do you dwell on the negative aspects? Let's take a closer look at your life.

- What are some of the benefits that have come your way in life?

- Are you allowing a few negatives to eclipse the many positives?

- How's your expectation level? Are you a realist or an idealist?

- What are some specific steps you can take in order to become a more positive person in the weeks ahead?

Enduring Grief's Grip

Genesis 23

The Washington Monument, stretching its single spire in a simple, proud silhouette against the sky. The Lincoln Memorial, forever gaunt and stately. The Jefferson Memorial . . . the Vietnam Memorial . . . stand as silent sentinels of our heritage. Reminders, lest we forget the patriotism and great contributions heroic people have made to our nation. They cast a shadow longer than our own lives. They help us look back. They help us look at and beyond ourselves.

The Old Testament, too, is full of memorials. There are sections of Chronicles and Kings that even seem like obituaries. Some of the names are hard to pronounce; sometimes only half a verse is given to their memory. But other times the Holy Spirit lingers like a bereaved mourner over one name or one death or one monument for a full chapter. And it's such chapters that command our full attention.

The twenty-third chapter of Genesis is one of those. It's a monument to Sarah, tucked between the pages of Abraham's story. It's like a moment of silence in the middle of a busy day. And it deserves, like a gravesite or memorial, not analysis but quiet reflection.

Before contemplating Sarah's memorial, though, let's address how we might respond to an announcement of impending death.

I. Stages of Grief We Often Grapple With

Death elicits deep feelings that we are often not prepared to handle. Instead of suppressing such feelings, we need to allow expression of our emotions through the grieving process. Elisabeth Kübler-Ross points out the stages of grief.[1]

A. Denial and isolation. "No, this can't be true!" We resist the message of imminent death, and begin to remove ourselves from others.

B. Anger. When reality settles in, rage and resentment scream, Why me? Like the rumblings of a volcano, questions and fury churn within us.

C. Bargaining. We feel that perhaps if we do enough good things, God will turn the tide of this terrible experience and make it go away. We try to make deals with God: "I'll dedicate my life to You . . . I'll go into Your service . . . I'll do whatever You want."

---

1. See *On Death and Dying,* by Elisabeth Kübler-Ross (New York, N.Y.: The Macmillan Co., 1969), pp. 38, 50, 82, 85, 112, 138. See also *Through the Valley of Tears: Encouragement and Guidance for the Bereaved,* by Cyril J. Barber and Sharalee Aspenleiter (Old Tappan, N.J.: Fleming H. Revell Co., 1987), pp. 27–39.

D. Depression. Eventually, hopelessness and depression take over, stealing our appetites and robbing us of sleep. Accompanying these feelings is a loss of purpose, lack of interest in life, and preoccupation with the one who is gone.

E. Acceptance. Perhaps a better word is resignation. It's not usually a relief from the sadness or an entrance of happiness; it's simply an acknowledgment of what has happened, an acceptance of the facts as they are.

F. Hope. Somehow the grace and mercy of God come to our rescue and give us the ability to go on. He restores purpose and meaning to our lives—rebuilds our lifeline of hope.

II. Abraham's Loss and Subsequent Sorrow

The woman who had shared Abraham's life—his departures and arrivals, gains and losses, highs and lows, encouragements and corrections, promises and disappointments—is gone.

A. The dying (vv. 1–2a). Scripture is so Spartan at times. We're not told how Sarah dies—she may have been ill for a long time, her body wracked with pain and suffering, or she could have passed quietly in her sleep. However, all we know is her age and the place of her death.

> Now Sarah lived one hundred and twenty-seven years; these were the years of the life of Sarah. And Sarah died in Kiriath-arba (that is, Hebron) in the land of Canaan.

Our last reference to Abraham and Sarah's place of residence was in Genesis 22:19. At that point, they were living in Beersheba. If Sarah was 90 when Isaac was born and about 110 when he was offered on the altar, that leaves seventeen years for her and Abraham to move—perhaps several times—and finally end up back in Canaan where she died.

B. The mourning (v. 2b). "Abraham went in to mourn for Sarah and to weep for her."[2] The verbs are strong in imagery: *mourn* means "to beat the breast" and *weep* means to "lament with grievous sorrow."

> ┌─ *A Time to Mourn* ─────────────────────────────
> Abraham's expression of grief was unrestrained and unapologetic. Some of us today, however, feel guilt over our grief. We want to rush past the deaths of our loved ones, to recover quickly and go on with life. We feel that

2. One scholar believes Abraham was not present when Sarah died. The verb "went in" is normally translated "came"; that is, Abraham "came" to Sarah's side after she died. See H. C. Leupold's *Exposition of Genesis* (Grand Rapids, Mich.: Baker Book House, 1942), vol. 2, p. 642.

it is somehow unspiritual to mourn. But Scripture never condemns grief. Tears are valuable. They are God-given relief mechanisms.

There are some who chide tears as unmanly, unsubmissive, unchristian. They would comfort us with a chill and pious stoicism, bidding us meet the most agitating passages of our history with rigid and tearless countenance. With such the spirit of the Gospel, and of the Bible, has little sympathy. We have no sympathy with a morbid sentimentality; but we may well question whether the man who cannot weep can really love; for sorrow is love, widowed and bereaved—and where that is present, its most natural expression is in tears. Religion does not come to make us unnatural and inhuman; but to purify and ennoble all those natural emotions with which our manifold nature is endowed. Jesus wept. Peter wept. The Ephesian converts wept on the neck of the Apostle whose face they thought they were never to see again. Christ stands by each mourner, saying, "Weep, my child; weep, for I have wept."

Tears relieve the burning brain, as a shower the electric clouds. Tears discharge the insupportable agony of the heart, as an overflow lessens the pressure of the flood against the dam. Tears are the material out of which heaven weaves its brightest rainbows.[3]

Abraham wept too. Leave room for weeping, not only in your life, but also in the lives of others.

C. The burying place (vv. 3–18). Abraham—a nomad, not a property owner—has to find a place to bury Sarah. So he approaches his neighbors, the Hittites. The graciousness of their response is customary in that region even today.

Then Abraham rose from before his dead, and spoke to the sons of Heth, saying, "I am a stranger and a sojourner among you; give me a burial site among you, that I may bury my dead out of my sight." (vv. 3–4)

3. F. B. Meyer, *Abraham; or, The Obedience of Faith* (1968; reprint, Fort Washington, Pa.: Christian Literature Crusade, 1971), p. 142.

The Hittites respond with respect.

"Hear us, my lord, you are a mighty prince among us;
bury your dead in the choicest of our graves; none
of us will refuse you his grave for burying your dead."
(v. 6)

Abraham desires two things: to bury Sarah where they have
been living and ministering, and to pay for the place of burial.
Abraham has put some thought to his needs. As difficult as it is
for him to work through the details, he knows he cannot pre-
sume upon these people for a gift. Instead, he follows the proper
procedures for obtaining property. The transaction is carried
out publicly and in the correct manner, fully attested to and put
on record. Ephron, however, interrupts.

"No, my lord, hear me; I give you the field, and I give
you the cave that is in it. In the presence of the sons
of my people I give it to you; bury your dead." (v. 11)

But Abraham insists on buying it. He wants a permanent record
among the Hittites that the property has been purchased, because he has plans for it for his family. Ephron, consequently,
works out a price.

"My lord, listen to me; a piece of land worth four
hundred shekels of silver,[4] what is that between me
and you? So bury your dead." And Abraham listened
to Ephron; and Abraham weighed out for Ephron the
silver which he had named in the hearing of the sons
of Heth, four hundred shekels of silver, commercial
standard. So Ephron's field, which was in Machpelah,
which faced Mamre, the field and cave which was in
it, and all the trees which were in the field, that were
within all the confines of its border, were deeded
over to Abraham for a possession in the presence of
the sons of Heth, before all who went in at the gate
of his city. And after this, Abraham buried Sarah his
wife in the cave of the field at Machpelah facing
Mamre (that is, Hebron) in the land of Canaan. So
the field, and the cave that is in it, were deeded over
to Abraham for a burial site by the sons of Heth.
(vv. 15–20)

And so, the burial site becomes a memorial.

---

4. The commercial standard for a silver shekel was .4 ounces, amounting to 160 ounces of
silver Abraham paid for the land. See *The Eerdmans Bible Dictionary* (Grand Rapids, Mich.:
William B. Eerdmans Publishing Co., 1987), p. 1053.

Neither Abraham nor the Hittites knew how significant
the sale of Machpelah was to become. It would be the
burial site not only of Sarah, but also of Abraham himself—
as well as Isaac, Rebekah, Leah (49:31), and Jacob (50:13).
Machpelah became a monument to the faith of great men
and women whose lives were clearly interwoven with the
God of Abraham.

III. Going Through and Getting Beyond Grief

There is not, in all of life, a deeper valley that we must walk through
than the death, mourning, burial, and grieving of a loved one. Here
are a few thoughts to hold onto when you go down that dark path.

A. Accept reality. Death is a reality all of us must face. Everything living must someday die. Since this is true, learn to hold
your relationships as God's gifts to you, to be enjoyed for a
season.

B. Grieve fully. Express the deep sadness. Let the tears flow. Talk
about your loss . . . don't be ashamed of it. And don't hurry
through the painful days. Give yourself permission to grieve fully.

C. Plan thoughtfully. Abraham gave thought to his plans for
Sarah's burial. When it's your turn to plan, make preparations
that will leave you satisfied. A life that has made an impact is
too significant to be quickly laid aside in a haphazard manner.

D. Communicate clearly. Do you have preferences about your
own funeral? Have you thought about what you'd like your epitaph to read? About your manner of burial? Talk over these
things with those closest to you.

E. Value dignity. A burial is a statement—a lasting memory, like
a baptism or a wedding. It is a ceremony, a reflection, a celebration of a life. And it can be not only a memorial for the one
you love, but a message of hope for others.

Living Insights

Study One ■■

This study surfaces an issue that isn't studied much: how death is
handled in the Scriptures. We've seen Abraham lose Sarah . . . the dying,
the mourning, the burying. Let's page through our Bibles to discover
additional insights in this area. In death, there are lessons to be learned.

- Study how death was handled both in the Old Testament and the New Testament. Use the following chart to record your observations. Look at the deaths of Joseph, Moses, Absalom, Lazarus, and Christ.

A Biblical Look at Dealing with Death	
Verses	Observations

Living Insights

We don't know if Sarah discussed her wishes for her burial with Abraham or not. But we do know that Abraham had some choices to make when she died, as we all do at the death of a loved one: where that person should be buried, what type of service to have, which songs to sing, who should perform the service. And those choices are made easier when we know what the person would have wanted. Have you given careful thought to what you want your funeral to be like? Do those close to you know your wishes? It's easy to put off thinking about such issues, but it's better to plan ahead.

- Have a frank discussion with your family about funerals, burials, ceremonies, and memorials. Explain your preferences in these areas. This doesn't have to be a morbid discussion. It can be a time of hope and dignity.

On Finding the Right Mate
Genesis 24

Socrates, the Greek philosopher, reportedly told his male students: "By all means marry. If you get a good wife, twice blessed will you be. If you get a bad wife, you will become a philosopher!"[1] Therefore, according to this philosopher, who you marry is not important, because the end results will be good. However, Abraham's approach did not follow this pattern. Unlike Socrates, his care reflects the value he placed on obtaining the right kind of marriage partner for his son.

Why all the fuss about how one seeks a wife? Simple. If we adopt methods that clash and clang, rather than hum and sing, we leap before looking, and pay sad consequences later.

I. Haphazard Methods for Choosing a Mate
Most people use one of three methods for choosing a marriage partner.

A. The fleshly method. Shape, size, looks, personality—the external image is the most important consideration. The trademark of this approach is using cleverness and manipulation to gain one's ends, at the expense of discernment and love.

B. The super spiritual method. This approach leaves it all in God's hands, taking no personal initiative or responsibility. The participants see even minute coincidences as signs from God. They rarely spend sufficient time together to be able to make a rational decision, but simply go "on faith" that God has intended them to be together.

C. The simple, natural method. This could be renamed the "take what you can get" approach—it happens most often in small communities or schools where there simply aren't many people to choose from. Settling for the available does not necessarily mean choosing the best.

> ┌─ *On Your Toes* ─────────────────────────────
> Even though we can improve our chances of finding a good mate by using biblical principles, no method of choosing a partner is free from risk. As long as there are choices to be made, it is possible to misjudge. And even when we've made a good choice, we still find ourselves married to someone with faults and weaknesses. There's

---

1. Socrates, as quoted by Dwight Hervey Small, in *Design for Christian Marriage* (Westwood, N. J.: Fleming H. Revell Co., 1959), p. 17.

just no such thing as a marriage without struggles. James Dobson tells a story that every married person will, at some point, identify with.

I received a classic letter recently from a woman who described an event that occurred during her first year of marriage. She and her husband became aware that a mouse was cohabiting their apartment—a concept which the woman found intolerable. Her husband set a trap to catch the furry little rodent, and soon did so. However, the type of cage that he constructed permitted them to capture the creature alive, presenting the question, "What do we do with him now?" Neither husband nor wife had the courage to murder the mouse in cold blood, but they didn't want to let him go, either. They finally settled on a solution. They would drown him.

The husband filled a bucket with water and carefully placed the cage, mouse included, into the liquid. The couple then left home for two hours, so as not to witness the final struggle. But when they returned, they found that the water didn't quite cover the top of the cage. The mouse had made the same discovery, and managed to keep the tip of his nose above the surface by standing on one toe.

I never learned how the final execution was administered. You see, the wife told me the story not to acquaint me with the plight of her mouse, but to illustrate her *own* difficulties. She said that the rodent, standing on one aching toe, came to symbolize her first year of marriage. She survived, but only by stretching to keep her nose above water.[2]

At one time or another, every marriage has found itself on one toe. But if you make an impulsive or improvident choice of a mate, you could be gasping for air for a long time to come.

2. James C. Dobson, *Straight Talk to Men and Their Wives* (Waco, Tex.: Word Books, 1980), pp. 113–14.

II. Reliable Principles for Choosing a Mate

The single most important decision you will ever make, apart from faith in Christ, is the selection of your life's mate. It's better to stay single than to rush into marriage out of loneliness or social pressure. Yet, although Scripture has a great deal to say about marriage, it devotes only one full chapter to the process of finding a mate— Genesis 24. And even in this chapter, the one who needs a mate isn't the one who's doing the searching. Abraham, according to the custom of the day, is seeking a wife for Isaac. Though traditions are different today, the principles we learn from this passage span the centuries.

A. Hear and heed counsel of godly parents (vv. 1–9). The first verse of Genesis 24 clues us in to the setting.

> Now Abraham was old, advanced in age; and the Lord
> had blessed Abraham in every way.

Here is a man who is between 120 and 135 years of age. Like most parents, he'd like to see his son happily married. But in this case, marriage is even more important than usual; for it's through Isaac's descendants that Israel will be blessed. So Abraham assigns his servant to the task. Notice the care with which Abraham gives the charge.

> And Abraham said to his servant, the oldest of his
> household, who had charge of all that he owned,
> "Please place your hand under my thigh,[3] and I will
> make you swear by the Lord, the God of heaven and
> the God of earth, that you shall not take a wife for
> my son from the daughters of the Canaanites, among
> whom I live, but you shall go to my country and to
> my relatives, and take a wife for my son Isaac." . . .
> So the servant placed his hand under the thigh of
> Abraham his master, and swore to him concerning
> this matter. (vv. 2–4, 9)

Listen to Your Parents

The godly counsel of loving parents is a jewel God has given you. Treasure it. Clutch it tightly. After all, they have

---

3. The underside of the thigh was regarded as the "seat of procreative power," according to William Gesenius, in *A Hebrew and English Lexicon of the Old Testament,* ed. Francis Brown in cooperation with S. R. Driver and Charles A. Briggs, trans. Edward Robinson (1907; reprint, London, England: Oxford University Press, Amen House, 1962), p. 438. The oath symbolized the binding of all future descendants to take vengeance should the agreement be broken. Some commentators feel the oath emphasizes circumcision and the covenant between God and the Israelites. See C. F. Keil and F. Delitzsch's *Biblical Commentary on the Old Testament* (Grand Rapids, Mich.: William B. Eerdmans Publishing Co., n.d.), vol. 1, pp. 257–58.

walked with the Lord quite a while longer than you have. And in some ways, they probably know you better than you know yourself. They're often more objective than you are, and less impulsive; and in many cases, they seem to have a sort of sixth sense about what's best for you. Parents are not always right. But their advice is certainly worth serious consideration, because they care about you. As we shall see, Isaac's father sought his well-being.

B. Saturate the whole process in prayer (vv. 10–14). Abraham's servant went about his assignment in a careful, sensitive, quiet manner. And most importantly, he prayed.

> "O Lord, the God of my master Abraham, please grant me success today, and show lovingkindness to my master Abraham. Behold, I am standing by the spring, and the daughters of the men of the city are coming out to draw water; now may it be that the girl to whom I say, 'Please let down your jar so that I may drink,' and who answers, 'Drink, and I will water your camels also';—may she be the one whom Thou hast appointed for Thy servant Isaac; and by this I shall know that Thou hast shown lovingkindness to my master." (vv. 12–14)

Certainly God wants us to evaluate a potential partner through the lens of Scripture. Specific prayer sensitizes our inner spirit to God, giving us resolve to wait and allow God to lead.

C. Look for qualities that reveal character (vv. 15–20). Long after physical beauty fades, character qualities remain. Abraham's servant observed Rebekah's inner beauty.

> And it came about before he had finished speaking, that behold, Rebekah who was born to Bethuel the son of Milcah, the wife of Abraham's brother Nahor, came out with her jar on her shoulder. And the girl was very beautiful, a virgin, and no man had had relations with her; and she went down to the spring and filled her jar, and came up. Then the servant ran to meet her, and said, "Please let me drink a little water from your jar." And she said, "Drink, my lord"; and she quickly lowered her jar to her hand, and gave him drink. . . . So she quickly emptied her jar into the trough, and ran back to the well to draw, and she drew for all his camels. (vv. 15–18, 20)

Several things commend Rebekah. She has genealogical solidarity—she comes from good roots. While she is physically beautiful, she's even lovelier within. Possessed by a pure and gracious sensitivity to others' needs, she quickly attends to the servant and even goes beyond his requests. Faithfulness, determination, diligence, tactfulness, hospitality, thoughtfulness, and compassion—Rebekah's strong character qualifies her as an excellent marital candidate for Isaac.

D. Study silently, think deeply, and proceed cautiously (vv. 21–27). Reflectively, Abraham's servant watches Rebekah closely as she tends to his needs (v. 21). Then he asks a question that will fill in the information gaps.

> "Whose daughter are you? Please tell me, is there room for us to lodge in your father's house?" (v. 23)

Her answer satisfies him.

> "I am the daughter of Bethuel, the son of Milcah, whom she bore to Nahor." Again she said to him, "We have plenty of both straw and feed, and room to lodge in." (vv. 24–25)

This man had asked God to lead him to the right girl. He had prayed . . . waited . . . evaluated. And now he is confident that God has answered.

> Then the man bowed low and worshiped the Lord. And he said, "Blessed be the Lord, the God of my master Abraham, who has not forsaken His lovingkindness and His truth toward my master; as for me, the Lord has guided me in the way to the house of my master's brothers." (vv. 26–27)

E. Notice relationships among immediate family members (vv. 28–32). Right away, Rebekah shares this encounter with her family (v. 28), and the servant has a chance to see the hospitality, openness, and freedom in their responses, especially of her brother Laban.

> And he [Laban] said, "Come in, blessed of the Lord! Why do you stand outside since I have prepared the house, and a place for the camels?" So the man entered the house. Then Laban unloaded the camels, and he gave straw and feed to the camels, and water to wash his feet and the feet of the men who were with him. (vv. 31–32)

Check the Roots

If there is pressure and trouble within your fiance's family, the chances are greater that your marriage will carry the same tone. When considering a partner, look for sibling harmony and parental respect. Is there open

---

communication among family members? Do fun and freedom characterize family gatherings? Are outsiders warmly
welcomed? Do they take time to talk—to share honestly?
Are they sensitive to one another's needs?

Your partner's family health is an indicator of your
future.

**F. Determine whether there is mutual interest in spiri-
tual things** (vv. 33–60). Abraham's servant cannot eat without
telling these people why he has come (vv. 33–38). As he finishes
his dramatic story, he turns to them and asks a penetrating
question.

> "So now if you are going to deal kindly and truly with
> my master, tell me; and if not, let me know, that I
> may turn to the right hand or the left." (v. 49)

Their response is positive.

> Then Laban and Bethuel answered and said, "The
> matter comes from the Lord; so we cannot speak to
> you bad or good. Behold, Rebekah is before you, take
> her and go, and let her be the wife of your master's
> son, as the Lord has spoken." (vv. 50–51)

Both Abraham's servant and Laban acknowledge the Lord's involvement in the process—they are in direct touch with the
living God. Yet there is genuine concern for Rebekah's feelings.

> And they said, "We will call the girl and consult her
> wishes." Then they called Rebekah and said to her,
> "Will you go with this man?" And she said, "I will go."
> (vv. 57–58)

She, too, understood God's purposes and submitted herself to
them, thereby proving her spiritual keenness.

G. Establish a solid foundation for marriage (vv. 61–67).
Healthy dating relationships are important. Keep in touch with
your emotions as you relate to a potential partner. Four ele-
ments stand out as important.

1. Wholesome anticipation. Both partners should be looking
forward to their union. Rebekah leaves her home and family
willingly (vv. 58, 61). And when Isaac sees the procession
on the horizon, his heart races (vv. 62–63). There should be
the beginnings of closeness between an engaged couple . . .
intimacy coupled with wholesome innocence. And there
should be an eager yearning for their marriage.

2. Reciprocal expectations. Isaac and Rebekah set out to
meet one another. There is mutual participation. A healthy
relationship involves both partners contributing to one

another's well-being. Something's wrong when a relationship is one-sided. When one partner has to bait the other, pull the other along, it's time to stop and reconsider.

3. **Open and unguarded communication.** When Isaac and Rebekah finally meet, Isaac listens to the servant share how God has worked to bring them together (v. 66). Information is freely shared. Of course, there is a cultural difference here—Isaac accepted his father's servant's choice for him, while we, on the other hand, are more directly involved in the choice of a partner. Nevertheless, communication is always important in any relationship. If you have difficulty communicating with your potential mate, that person may very well not be the one for you.

4. **Intimate, comforting affection.** Isaac and Rebekah developed a reassuring intimacy.

> Then Isaac brought her into his mother Sarah's tent, and he took Rebekah, and she became his wife; and he loved her; thus Isaac was comforted after his mother's death. (v. 67)

III. Some "Always" and "Nevers" We Need to Remember
Courtship and marriage can be a rocky road. Here are a few rules for the road to help you avoid the potholes.

A. **Always pursue God's will with greater intensity than your own.** Force yourself to connect with the living Lord. Pray for restraint from moving ahead of God. You'll need the Lord to give you the right timing in the decisions you make.

B. **Always be honest throughout your courtship and marriage.** Be truthful; do not be afraid to share your likes and dislikes. Pay attention to your doubts—you may be heading for something not intended for you.

C. **Never rush into anything that may lead to permanence.** Take the necessary time to consider all of your feelings and concerns.

D. **Never rationalize away the importance of sexual purity.** Never grant yourself privileges God forbids. Guidelines are for your well-being.

Living Insights

Study One

Genesis 24 is a unique chapter in the Bible. It centers around the search for Isaac's life partner. Let's walk through this chapter wisely and carefully.

- Our study centers around seven reliable principles for choosing a mate. Let's personalize the first three. Reread the passages below and ask yourself the following questions:

What does it say?
What does it mean?
What does it mean to me?
What does it mean to those in my family?

—Hear and heed counsel of godly parents (24:1–9).
—Saturate the whole process in prayer (vv. 10–14).
—Look for qualities that reveal character (vv. 15–20).

 Living Insights

Study Two ━━━

Let's continue our study of Genesis 24. Look at the last four principles for choosing a mate. Reread the accompanying texts and ask yourself the same questions you did in Study One.

—Study silently, think deeply, and proceed cautiously (24:21–27).
—Notice relationships among immediate family members (vv. 28–32).
—Determine whether there is mutual interest in spiritual things (vv. 33–60).
—Establish a solid foundation for marriage (vv. 61–67).

What a Way to Go!
Genesis 25:1–10

Most of us can relate to Flip Wilson's famous sentiment that if we had our entire lives to live over again, we doubt we'd have the strength.

Life can be exhausting. The closer we come to the end of our lives, the better retirement starts to look. We begin to have visions of ourselves all alone on a shady back porch—just us and a rocker and a tall glass of ice tea. No jangling telephones, no noisy teenagers, no demanding work schedule. Just a sunset and some quiet music as we go trailing off into the twilight years of our lives.

Pretty appealing picture, isn't it?

But aren't the very things that exhaust us the ones that bring fulfillment? What could be more satisfying than sinking into bed, tired from a day's work well done? Or knowing your kids need you? Or feeling the ache of creative muscles stretched to capacity?

Active participation in life is exhilarating. It's the mundane that wears us out and builds the illusion that retirement offers a step up in life when in fact it may be a step down.

When daily routine bores you silly, it's time to examine your priorities. Where do you *really* want to be at the end of your life? Propped on a porch with a Do Not Disturb sign on the door...or smack in the middle of exuberant existence? Let's see what lessons along these lines we can learn from Abraham's final days.

I. Common Misconceptions of the Twilight Years
Most people approach retirement with one of three faulty ideas.
   A. Narcissism. This thinking proclaims, "Leave me alone. I've earned the right to my own privacy...my own little world. I've done my job. I've paid my dues. I deserve to live for myself." Narcissism is a preoccupation with self, common among those who are tired of coping with life.
   B. Pessimism. This notion moans, "I have nothing more to contribute—I'm too old, and no one cares anyway. I've been kicked out of society." This negativism grows into a decision to quit—to just pull out of life into despondency.
   C. Fatalism. This sentiment sighs, "Why can't I just die? I have made my contribution...all that is in front of me is the grave!" This person doesn't want to face failing health and energy.

"Advice to a (Bored) Young Man"

For some folks life is filled with curiosities and mysteries that need solving. And with endless energy they seek to unravel the enigmas that surround them—they are adventurous people. An article in *Newsweek* titled "Advice to a (Bored) Young Man" sheds light on the life of one individual whose twilight years continued a lifetime of exploration and discovery.

Died, age 20; buried, age 60. The sad epitaph of too many Americans. Mummification sets in on too many young men at an age when they should be ripping the world wide open. For example: Many people reading this page are doing so with the aid of bifocals. Inventor? *B. Franklin,* age 79.

The presses that printed this page were powered by electricity. One of the first harnessers? *B. Franklin,* age 40.

Some are reading this on the campus of one of the Ivy League universities. Founder? *B. Franklin,* age 45.

Others, in a library. Who founded the first library in America? *B. Franklin,* age 25. . . .

Now, think fire. Who started the first fire department, invented the lightning rod, designed a heating stove still in use today? *B. Franklin,* ages 31, 43, 36.

Wit. Conversationalist. Economist. Philosopher. Diplomat. Printer. Publisher. Linguist (spoke and wrote five languages). Advocate of paratroopers (from balloons) a century before the airplane was invented. All this until age 84.

And he had exactly two years of formal schooling. It's a good bet that you already have more sheer knowledge than Franklin ever had when he was your age.

Perhaps you think there's no use trying to think of anything new, that everything's been done. Wrong. The simple, agrarian America of Franklin's day didn't begin to need the answers we need today.

Go do something about it.[1]

1. As quoted in *Motivation to Last a Lifetime,* by Ted W. Engstrom (Grand Rapids, Mich.: Zondervan Publishing House, 1984), pp. 23–24.

II. Abraham: An Uncommon Example

Abraham is that rare example of someone who lived life to the hilt, right up to the end of his life. His biblical biography doesn't even begin until he's 75! And his life was one adventure after another for one hundred years after that. There's no squeak of a rocking chair here. Instead, what we hear are wedding bells!

A. His new wife (Gen. 25:1). After Sarah's death and Isaac's marriage (chaps. 23–24), Abraham marries again.

> Now Abraham took another wife, whose name was Keturah. (25:1)

Instead of asking why Abraham would marry again at his age—probably around 125—a better question would be, why not? He'd had a wonderful relationship with Sarah. He loved his home, loved having a family. And he had grown accustomed to the intimate companionship of a mate. So when Sarah died, remarriage became a choice to consider.

B. His second family (vv. 2–4). Abraham doesn't stop with getting another wife. Keturah bears him children—six of them!

> And she [Keturah] bore to him Zimran and Jokshan and Medan and Midian and Ishbak and Shuah. (v. 2)

Read this too quickly and you gloss over fifty-four months of pregnancy. Abraham, at age 125, is starting a whole new family; he's surrounded by preschoolers! The passage even goes on to list the names of Abraham's second set of grandchildren.

> And Jokshan became the father of Sheba and Dedan. And the sons of Dedan were Asshurim and Letushim and Leummim. And the sons of Midian were Ephah and Epher and Hanoch and Abida and Eldaah. All these were the sons of Keturah. (vv. 3–4)

So far there is no sign of any deterioration of Abraham's love or zest for life.

Retired . . . or Refired?

God's plan reaches far beyond retirement. Your occupation, though a major part of your life, may be just a preparation for your later years. You may not have a second family as Abraham did, but if your mentality is to fire up instead of tire out, you may find yourself on the cutting edge of something wonderful and fulfilling in your twilight years.

C. His generous inheritance (vv. 5–6). Abraham, a responsible father, makes plans for the distribution of his wealth.

Now Abraham gave all that he had to Isaac; but to
the sons of his concubines, Abraham gave gifts while
he was still living, and sent them away from his son
Isaac eastward, to the land of the east. (vv. 5–6)

Even though Abraham's will is written, he doesn't bundle everything up for later. He wants some of it to be enjoyed while he's
still alive.

--- **Plan Ahead** ---

In our selfish society, it's easy to buy into the mentality
that we should live only for today and let our kids take
care of their future by themselves. But the Bible says the
opposite.

Children are not responsible to save up for their
parents, but parents for their children. (2 Cor.
12:14b)

Consider what it would mean to your children if you
had a legally signed will and an adequate insurance pack-
age. Your care for your family can extend far beyond your
death. And not just monetarily. What kind of emotional
and spiritual inheritance are you laying up for them? Are
you involved in making life a little brighter, happier, and
more fulfilling for your family? Are they enjoying the fruits
of your labor? Are they learning generosity through your
example? Lasting impressions linger in the minds of people
who benefit from a generous, godly hand.

D. His final departure (Gen. 25:7–10). What a way to go!
Abraham has enjoyed a new wife and family, his house is in
order, and he has a wealth of meaningful memories.

And these are all the years of Abraham's life that
he lived, one hundred and seventy-five years. And
Abraham breathed his last and died in a ripe old age,
an old man and satisfied with life. (vv. 7–8a)

"An old man and satisfied with life." He had thrown himself into
life as God presented it to him and found it extremely rewarding.
Young at heart, he found no room for a crotchety or bitter attitude. His love for God superseded the hardships he experienced.
Everything he did had the final signature of satisfaction upon it.

Then his sons Isaac and Ishmael buried him in the
cave of Machpelah, in the field of Ephron the son
of Zohar the Hittite, facing Mamre, the field which
Abraham purchased from the sons of Heth; there
Abraham was buried with Sarah his wife. (vv. 9–10)

What are you doing right now to stay young, vibrant, romantic, fulfilled, satisfied, interested, growing, learning? What stimulating books are you reading this week? What conversations do you have with people who prod your thinking? How much room do you have for disagreements and negotiations in your life? Do you include others in your family circle? How much effort do you exert to reach out to those that you've not met before? How much of your day is spent in laughter, fun, and enjoyment?

Abraham's life answered these questions in a positive, satisfying way. How does your life measure up by comparison?

III. Two Essentials for Finishing Well

There are lots of quick starters in life, but few are strong finishers. Here are some tips for staying in the race.

A. Remember that each day offers opportunities for staying young at heart. Claim them! For example, you can choose your attitudes; you can choose how to invest your time—in reading widely and wisely, in helping others, in making plans; you can choose to be involved in activities, to have a sense of humor. Life isn't over. You just have to make the most of it! Denis Waitley mentions "ten action reminders" for staying motivated.[2]

1. Wake up happy.
2. Use positive self-talk from morning to bedtime.
3. Look at problems as opportunities.
4. Concentrate all your energy and intensity without distraction on the successful completion of your current, most important project.
5. Find something good in all of your personal relationships and accentuate the blessings or lessons in even the most trying confrontations.
6. Learn to stay relaxed and friendly no matter how much tension you are under.
7. Think and speak well of your health.
8. Expect the best from others, too!
9. This week seek and talk in person to someone who is currently doing what you want to do most and doing it well.
10. The best way to remain optimistic is to associate with . . . optimists.

2. Denis Waitley, as quoted in *Motivation to Last a Lifetime,* by Engstrom, pp. 50–51.

B. Refuse to give up—right to the very end. Winston Churchill, the man who saw England through the dark and difficult years of World War II, gave one of the briefest and most profound speeches in history when he returned to the school that had trained him.

> Never give in, never give in, never, never, never, never—in nothing, great or small, large or petty—never give in except to convictions of honor and good sense.[3]

Let that be your motto. Never give in—ever—unless honor and good sense tap you on the shoulder.

 Living Insights

Study One ▬▬▬▬▬▬▬▬▬▬▬▬▬▬▬▬▬▬▬▬▬▬▬▬▬▬▬▬▬▬▬

We're quickly bringing our biographical study of Abraham to a close, and a review now might help us cement the things we have learned so far.

- Listed below are the titles of the first twelve lessons. Go back through your Bible, your study guide, and your notes in order to summarize one key biblical truth you learned in each of those lessons.

Key Biblical Truths

The Man Who Pioneered Faith _____

_____

Going . . . Not Knowing _____

_____

Maintaining Vital Contact _____

_____

When the Godly Slump _____

_____

Continued on next page

---

3. Winston Churchill, as quoted in *Bartlett's Familiar Quotations,* 15th ed., rev. and enl. (Boston, Mass.: Little, Brown and Co., 1980), p. 745.

A Decision That Led to Disaster _____

_____

Abraham, the Greathearted _____

_____

A Vision, a Dialogue, a Covenant _____

_____

When You Run Ahead, *Watch Out!* _____

_____

The Joys of Walking with God _____

_____

One of Those Upper-Downer Days _____

_____

Understanding the Dynamics of Prayer _____

_____

When the Cesspool Overflows _____

_____

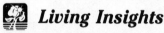 *Living Insights*

Study Two ▬▬▬▬▬▬▬▬▬▬▬▬▬▬▬▬▬▬▬▬▬▬▬

In this Living Insights, we want to review the applications we gleaned from the first twelve lessons in our series. It's the practical nature of this study that makes it so relevant.

• The list below is the same as that in Study One, with one exception. Here we are focusing on one key application discovered in each lesson. So page through your Bible and study guide once more and write down one application that you found helpful in your life.

Key Applications

The Man Who Pioneered Faith _____

_____

Portrait of a Saint . . .
Warts and All
Genesis 12–25

Oliver Cromwell, lord protector of seventeenth century England, had a unique character trait—though an important figure, he never became enamored with himself.

At the apex of his popularity, he reluctantly agreed to a portrait sitting, but not without these words to the artist:

> I desire you would use all your skill to paint my picture truly like me, and not flatter me at all; but remark all these rough-nesses, pimples, warts, and everything as you see me, otherwise I will never pay a farthing for it.[1]

In this day of air-brushed photographs, cosmetic surgery, and expensive makeup, it's refreshing to hear of someone who says, "Paint me, warts and all." The Bible gives us untouched portraits of great men and women whose flaws are not hidden. Abraham was one of these. Let's take a final look at this man and how his life can help us.

I. Some Benefits of Studying Biblical Biographies

If we could visit godly men and women whose names appear in Scripture, we would possibly find each saying candidly, "Spirit of God, tell them the truth—the whole truth—about both my dark and light sides. Let them see me as I am." Such biographies strengthen our stride as we walk with God.

A. Biographies translate truth into life. Truth remains sterile, abstract, and theoretical until it is wrapped in flesh and blood. For example, friendship becomes tangible in the face of Lazarus's emerging from the grave at the call of Christ. Suffering is merely a subject unless it's felt through the boils of Job, the thorn in Paul's flesh, or the dungeons where Joseph and Daniel spent sleepless nights.

B. Biographies give us a closer kinship with our "fathers in the faith." When we see how men and women of faith reacted to situations in their culture, we sense a oneness with them. Even though centuries separate us, we discover that people like Moses, Ruth, Elisha, and Rahab are very much like us—and we are drawn to them.

---

1. Oliver Cromwell, as quoted in *Bartlett's Familiar Quotations,* 15th ed., rev. and enl. (Boston, Mass.: Little, Brown and Co., 1980), p. 272.

C. Biographies stabilize us when we go through similar events. There is something about knowing you are not the first to lose a child, to face an angry superior, to struggle for a parent's approval, or to encounter ministry differences as Paul did with Barnabas. The lives of men and women of faith are recorded for our encouragement and stability. As Scripture tells us:

> For whatever was written in earlier times was written for our instruction, that through perseverance and the encouragement of the Scriptures we might have hope. (Rom. 15:4)

D. Biographies help us maintain a divine perspective. A close look at others' godly walks motivates us to follow their example. Finding them in prayer or standing alone in a decision or being willing to die for a cause puts fire in our bones. The Bible is filled with people whose lives cast shadows, some large and some small, across the biblical landscape. For example, only a few verses are devoted to Jabez's life, while a whole chapter opens Mephibosheth's story. Abraham, however, is given much more press. And, although the Bible paints its characters as people with natures just like ours (James 5:17)—warts and all—we can learn much from them. Even from their mistakes (1 Cor. 10:6, 11).

II. A Brief Overview of Abraham's Life

The story of Abraham's life is given in fourteen chapters in Genesis. As we review what we've learned, let's turn to Hebrews 11, where we find Abraham's faith being underscored throughout his life.

A. His heights. Several important pinnacles of success are visible as we scan the range of Abraham's life.

1. **When he was called, he obeyed.** There was no wrestling with God's call. He simply obeyed.

   > By faith Abraham, when he was called, obeyed by going out to a place which he was to receive for an inheritance; and he went out, not knowing where he was going. (Heb. 11:8)

   He responded to God's call even though he had no maps, travel agency, or motel accommodations to assist him.

2. **When he was promised, he believed.** Abraham took God's word literally.

   > By faith he lived as an alien in the land of promise, as in a foreign land, dwelling in tents with Isaac and Jacob, fellow heirs of the same promise; for he was looking for the city which has foundations, whose architect and builder is God. (vv. 9–10)

Paul also comments on Abraham's confidence in God.

> Yet, with respect to the promise of God, he did not waver in unbelief, but grew strong in faith, giving glory to God, and being fully assured that what He had promised, He was able also to perform. (Rom. 4:20–21)

3. **When he was tested, he trusted.** He never wavered in his faith.

> By faith Abraham, when he was tested, offered up Isaac; and he who had received the promises was offering up his only begotten son; it was he to whom it was said, "In Isaac your descendants shall be called." He considered that God is able to raise men even from the dead; from which he also received him back as a type. (Heb. 11:17–19)

He simply trusted that God knew what He was doing.

4. **When he was blessed, he shared.** Although God blessed Abraham with wealth, Abraham held his possessions loosely—even to the point of offering his best land to his nephew.

> Now Lot, who went with Abram, also had flocks and herds and tents. And the land could not sustain them while dwelling together; for their possessions were so great that they were not able to remain together. And there was strife between the herdsmen of Abram's livestock and the herdsmen of Lot's livestock. Now the Canaanite and the Perizzite were dwelling then in the land. Then Abram said to Lot, "Please let there be no strife between you and me, nor between my herdsmen and your herdsmen, for we are brothers. Is not the whole land before you? Please separate from me: if to the left, then I will go to the right; or if to the right, then I will go to the left." And Lot lifted up his eyes and saw all the valley of the Jordan, that it was well watered everywhere— this was before the Lord destroyed Sodom and Gomorrah—like the garden of the Lord, like the land of Egypt as you go to Zoar. (Gen. 13:5–10)

Abraham handled his wealth with an open hand. His eyes were not fixed on the material wealth God had given him (see Prov. 23:4–5).

5. **When he was burdened, he prayed.** Lot's choice of land put him on the verge of being destroyed with the sinful city

he'd chosen to live in. Abraham couldn't bear to see that happen, so he pleaded with God on his nephew's behalf.

And Abraham came near and said, "Wilt Thou indeed sweep away the righteous with the wicked? Suppose there are fifty righteous within the city; wilt Thou indeed sweep it away and not spare the place for the sake of the fifty righteous who are in it?" (Gen. 18:23–24)

When God called, Abraham obeyed. When God promised, Abraham believed. When God tested, Abraham trusted. When God blessed, Abraham shared. When God burdened, Abraham prayed.

B. His depths. Abraham's life is a timeless synonym for faith and stability. But he was not without his pimples and warts.

1. When he was afraid, he escaped. This was true geographically.

Now there was a famine in the land; so Abram went down to Egypt to sojourn there, for the famine was severe in the land. (12:10)

It was also true personally, when he lied about his relationship to Sarah to avoid trouble.

And it came about when he came near to Egypt, that he said to Sarai his wife, "See now, I know that you are a beautiful woman; and it will come about when the Egyptians see you, that they will say, 'This is his wife'; and they will kill me, but they will let you live. Please say that you are my sister so that it may go well with me because of you, and that I may live on account of you." (vv. 11–13)

2. When he was impatient, he heeded wrong counsel. God promised to give Abraham a son, but Abraham couldn't wait. He took the advice of his wife and fathered a child.

Now Sarai, Abram's wife had borne him no children, and she had an Egyptian maid whose name was Hagar. So Sarai said to Abram, "Now behold, the Lord has prevented me from bearing children. Please go in to my maid; perhaps I shall obtain children through her." And Abram listened to the voice of Sarai. (16:1–2)

3. When he failed, he didn't "break the bent" of lying under pressure. Abraham lied twice about his relationship to Sarah because he believed the men of the region would kill him so they could take his wife (chaps. 12, 20). Later, after Abraham had died, Isaac reenacted the same scenario. So Isaac lived in Gerar. When the men of the place asked about his wife, he said, "She is my sister," for he was afraid to say, "my wife," thinking, "the men of the place might kill me on account of Rebekah, for she is beautiful." (26:6–7) Abraham had not broken his own bent toward lying and, in turn, had passed the same trait on to his son. He failed to help Isaac see how misleading and deceitful he had been, not only with the people of the land, but also by placing his wife in a compromising position. So when his son found himself in a similar situation, he simply followed his father's example.

III. Some Practical Lessons to Be Learned

We can draw at least five lessons from our concluding study of Abraham's life. Although his warts are glaring and obvious, the finer features of his faith override a multitude of imperfections.

—Whenever God calls, obey.
—Whenever God promises, believe.
—Whenever God tests, trust.
—Whenever God blesses, share.
—Whenever God burdens, pray.

Living Insights

Let's continue our review of the lessons we've learned in our study of Abraham's life.

- The last twelve lesson titles in our series are listed below. Looking back over the material, pinpoint one key biblical truth you discovered in each lesson.

Key Biblical Truth

A Wail of Two Cities _____

_____

Ultimate Indecency _____

_____

Disobedience Déjà Vu _____

_____

It's a Boy! _____

_____

Domestic Disharmony _____

_____

A Well, a Tree, and a Covenant _____

_____

When God Says, "Let Go!" _____

_____

The Pleasures of Passing God's Exams _____

_____

Enduring Grief's Grip _____

_____

On Finding the Right Mate _____

_____

Continued on next page

What a Way to Go! _____

Portrait of a Saint ... Warts and All _____

![Living Insights icon] **Living Insights**

Our goal for the Living Insights has been to help you apply God's Word to your life. Have we been successful?

- Page back through your Bible and your study guide in an attempt to focus in on one application that you made from each of the last twelve lessons. Write your responses below.

Key Application

A Wail of Two Cities _____

_____

Ultimate Indecency _____

_____

Disobedience Déjà Vu _____

_____

It's a Boy! _____

_____

Domestic Disharmony _____

_____

A Well, a Tree, and a Covenant _____

_____

When God Says, "Let Go!" _____

_____

The Pleasures of Passing God's Exams _____

_____

A Patriarch in Panorama
The Life of Abraham
Genesis 12–25

Events	The Covenant The Departure The Famine	Return from Egypt Separation from Lot	War Declared Lot Delivered Reward Refused	Abrahamic Covenant Reaffirmed	Birth of Ishmael	Names Changed Circum-cision Instituted Isaac and Ishmael Discussed
Chapter	12	13	14	15	16	17
Period	75 years old (12:4)				86 years old (16:16)	99 years old (17:1)
Promise	Affirmed (12:1–3)	Reaffirmed (13:14–17)		Reaffirmed (Entire chapter)		Reaffirmed (17:1–14)
People	Abram, Sarai, Lot, Servants, Pharoah	Abram, Sarai, Lot	Heathen Kings, Abram, Lot, Melchizedek	Abram, God	Sarai, Abram, Hagar, Ishmael	Abraham, God
Place	Haran, Shechem, Moreh, Bethel, Ai to Egypt	Between Bethel and Ai, Hebron	Valley of Siddim, Hebron, Valley of Shaveh	Hebron (?)		

	18	19	20	21	22	23	24	25
	Promise of a Son	Sodom Destroyed	Abimelech	Isaac Born → Ishmael Cast Out	Isaac Offered	Sarah's Death and Burial	Isaac's Bride	Abraham's Second Marriage
	Plans for Destruction of Sodom	Lot Spared		Abimelech Reproved	Covenant Reaffirmed			Abraham's Death and Burial
			Abraham: 100 years old Sarah: 90 years old (17:17, 21:5)			Abraham: 137 years old (23:1)	"Old, advanced in age" (24:1)	175 years old (25:7)
					Reaffirmed (22:15–18)			
	Abraham, Three "Men" (Angels and God), Sarah	Two Angels, Lot and Family, Sodomites, Abraham	Abraham, Sarah, Abimelech	Sarah, Abraham, Isaac, Ishmael, Hagar, Abimelech	Abraham, Isaac, Angel of the Lord	Sarah, Abraham, Sons of Heth	Abraham, Eldest Servant, Rebekah, Isaac	Abraham, Keturah, Family, Isaac
	Hebron (Oaks of Mamre)	Sodom and Gomorrah, Mountain Cave	Gerar	Hebron (?), Beersheba, Paran	Moriah	Hebron, Field of Machpelah	Mesopotamia, Nahor	Cave in Field of Machpelah

Books for Probing Further

William Frederick Faber's love for God compelled him to pen praises to His various attributes. Enthralled with His mercy, he wrote, "There's a wideness in God's mercy."[1] When recognizing people's faith in God, generation after generation, he penned, "Faith of our fathers! living still."[2] And when he was overwhelmed by God's eternality—that God is now and forever—he wrote,

> Thou hast no youth, great God,
> An Unbeginning End Thou art;
> Thy glory in itself abode,
> And still abides in its own tranquil heart:
> No age can heap its outward years on Thee:
> Dear God! Thou art Thyself Thine own
> eternity.[3]

God's eternality envelops our world—now—where we work, play, raise our families, and interact with our neighbors. As now, so it was centuries ago when this majestic God revealed Himself to Abraham and redirected the remaining chapters of his life.

Today God still meets us where we are. And as He does, He woos us to Himself, just as He did Abraham. Get to know Abraham's God and take courage to follow Abraham's pilgrimage of faith. In order to do that our minds need to be stimulated to think about God and His ways. Therefore, several excellent books are suggested below to help you forge out a biblical understanding of God as you walk with Him.

I. Whenever God Calls, Obey

Howard, J. Grant. *Balancing Life's Demands: A New Perspective on Priorities.* Portland, Oreg.: Multnomah Press, 1983. Present demands sap our energies, and opportunities are allowed only a sideways squeeze into our already overbooked schedules. Often we make lists, only to have them mockingly stare back at us by the end of the day—undone. J. Grant Howard offers a fresh approach to personal organization by giving us a new perspective on priorities—a perspective that places *God* at the top of the list.

Piper, John. *Desiring God: Meditations of a Christian Hedonist.* Portland, Oreg.: Multnomah Press, 1986. Piper has slightly changed a

---

1. Frederick William Faber, "There's a Wideness in God's Mercy," from *The Hymnal for Worship and Celebration* (Waco, Tex.: Word Music, 1986), no. 68.

2. Faber, "Faith of Our Fathers," from *The Hymnal for Worship and Celebration,* no. 279.

3. Faber, as quoted in A. W. Tozer's *The Divine Conquest* (Harrisburg, Pa.: Christian Publications, 1950), p. 20.

classic catechistic teaching to read "The chief end of man is to glorify God *by* enjoying him forever" (emphasis added).[4] We can follow God with different motivations—guilt or a sense of obligation or fear of punishment. Piper suggests a stronger, more biblical motivation—that of *desiring* God.

Richards, Lawrence O. *A Practical Theology of Spirituality.* Grand Rapids, Mich.: Zondervan Publishing House, Academie Books, 1987. Richards spades our thinking like rich soil, preparing it to receive seeds of application in his exercises at the end of each chapter. While he does discuss the traditional views of spirituality, his main thrust is to expand the implications of a believer's union with God. In doing so, he encourages us to follow the living God where furrows of lush spiritual growth await us.

II. Whenever God Promises, Believe

Packer, J. I. *Knowing God.* Downers Grove, Ill.: InterVarsity Press, 1973. In this fine volume, Packer challenges us to rethink our perceptions of God. From this new well of thought, our spirits can drink, and we can then face the world with renewed vigor, courage, and peace.

Tozer, A. W. *The Knowledge of the Holy.* New York, N.Y.: Harper and Row, Publishers, 1961. Our confidence in God is directly related to our understanding of Him as a person, and Tozer puts knowing Him on an intensely practical level. As he says, "I believe there is scarcely an error in doctrine or a failure in applying Christian ethics that cannot be traced finally to imperfect and ignoble thoughts about God" (p. 10).

III. Whenever God Tests, Trust

Barber, Cyril J., and Sharalee Aspenleiter. *Through the Valley of Tears: Encouragement and Guidance for the Bereaved.* Old Tappan, N.J.: Fleming H. Revell Co., 1987. Abraham nearly lost his youngest son and later was bereaved of his wife. The pain and loneliness that accompany the death of a loved one may bring depression, anxiety, anger, and the numbing reality of having to begin again. The authors sensitively address immediate problems and offer long-range solutions.

---

4. John Piper, *Desiring God: Meditations of a Christian Hedonist* (Portland, Oreg.: Multnomah Press, 1986), p. 14. Westminster's *Shorter Catechism* answers the question, "What is the chief end of man?" with, "Man's chief end is to glorify God, and to enjoy him for ever." *The Shorter Catechism of the Westminster Assembly* (Philadelphia, Pa.: Board of Christian Education of the Presbyterian Church in the United States of America, n.d.), p. 5.

Seamands, David A. *Healing for Damaged Emotions*. Wheaton, Ill.: Scripture Press Publications, Victor Books, 1981. Abraham's strained relationship with his nephew Lot and the consequences of his alliance with Hagar left him emotionally vulnerable. Those like Abraham, who are stressed and scarred, will find this book a wellspring of hope and healing.

Streeter, Carole Sanderson. *Finding Your Place After Divorce*. Grand Rapids, Mich.: Zondervan Publishing House, Pyranee Books, 1986. Cast out from the safety and security of Abraham's house, Hagar knew separation's pain—a pain many divorcees feel. The author gently but pointedly discusses issues designed to help the divorcée piece together a foundation for life after divorce.

————. *Reflections for Women Alone*. Wheaton, Ill.: Scripture Press Publications, Victor Books, 1987. For women who are widowed, divorced, or single, this book will help you gain a stronger sense of personhood, belonging, and purpose. Even though Hagar was alone, God affirmed her person, position, and future. And He will do the same for you.

Swindoll, Charles R. *Three Steps Forward, Two Steps Back: Persevering Through Pressure*. Nashville, Tenn.: Thomas Nelson Publishers, 1980. Realistically written, this book offers refreshing encouragement for the fellow pilgrim struggling to trust God in the midst of testing.

IV. Whenever God Blesses, Share

Blue, Ron. *Master Your Money: A Step-by-step Plan for Financial Freedom*. Nashville, Tenn.: Thomas Nelson Publishers, 1986. Abraham was free to pull up his tent pegs and follow God because his tent wasn't mortgaged to the hilt. And as he was blessed by God, he in turn became a blessing to others—both spiritually and materially. This practical book offers hands-on counsel for those who need a workable plan to wisely manage their resources.

Inrig, Gary. *Quality Friendship*. Chicago, Ill.: Moody Press, 1981. In an age of superficial relationships, transparent expression is often left begging on the doorstep of unformed friendships, even in some churches and their programs. This is a book to help transform those tentative relationships into strong and enduring friendships.

V. Whenever God Burdens, Pray

White, John. *Daring to Draw Near: People in Prayer*. Downers Grove, Ill.: Inter-Varsity Press, 1977. In this book principles of prayer are drawn from the lives of biblical characters such as Jacob, Moses,

David, Daniel, Hannah, Job, Paul, and Jesus, with an especially intriguing chapter on Abraham. White draws us to the heart of these people to help us gaze on eternal issues of life and death. Their humanity assures that we, too, can dare to draw near to the eternal, holy God.

Acknowledgments

Insight for Living is grateful for permission to quote from the following sources:

Brasier, Virginia. "Time of the Mad Atom." Reprinted with permission of the Saturday Evening Post. Indianapolis, Ind.: The Curtis Publishing Co., 1949.

Dobson, James C. *Straight Talk to Men and Their Wives.* Waco, Tex.: Word Books, 1980.

Meyer, F. B. *Abraham; or, The Obedience of Faith.* Fort Washington, Pa.: Christian Literature Crusade, 1971.

Insight for Living
Cassette Tapes
ABRAHAM ... THE FRIEND OF GOD

Here is faith in action. Even though he lived in ancient times, Abraham modeled an enviable walk with his Lord—not perfect, but with a sincerity seldom found today. These studies will motivate you to replace theoretical talk about God with a practical walk with God.

			U.S.	Canada
ABE	CS	Cassette series—includes album cover	$65.25	$83.00
		Individual cassettes—include messages		
		A and B	5.00	6.35

These prices are effective as of September 1988 and are subject to change without notice.

ABE **1-A:** *The Man Who Pioneered Faith*—Genesis 11–13, 15, 17–18, 21–22, 25
B: *Going . . . Not Knowing*—Hebrews 11:8–10, Acts 7:2–7

ABE **2-A:** *Maintaining Vital Contact*—Genesis 12:1–9
B: *When the Godly Slump*—Genesis 12:10–20

ABE **3-A:** *A Decision That Led to Disaster*—Genesis 13
B: *Abraham, the Greathearted*—Genesis 14

ABE **4-A:** *A Vision, a Dialogue, a Covenant*—Genesis 15
B: *When You Run Ahead,* Watch Out!—Genesis 16

ABE **5-A:** *The Joys of Walking with God*—Genesis 17
B: *One of Those Upper-Downer Days*—Genesis 18

ABE **6-A:** *Understanding the Dynamics of Prayer*—James 4:2–3, Numbers 11:1–33, Genesis 18–19, Judges 16:26–30
B: *When the Cesspool Overflows*—Genesis 19:1–14

ABE **7-A:** *A Wail of Two Cities*—Genesis 19:15–29
B: *Ultimate Indecency*—Genesis 19:30–38

ABE **8-A:** *Disobedience Déjà Vu*—Genesis 20
B: *It's a Boy!*—Genesis 21:1–7

ABE **9-A:** *Domestic Disharmony*—Genesis 21:8–21
B: *A Well, a Tree, and a Covenant*—Genesis 21:22–34

ABE **10-A:** *When God Says, "Let Go!"*—Genesis 22:1–14
B: *The Pleasures of Passing God's Exams*—Genesis 22:11–19

ABE **11-A:** *Enduring Grief's Grip*—Genesis 23
B: *On Finding the Right Mate*—Genesis 24

ABE **12-A:** *What a Way to Go!*—Genesis 25:1–10
B: *Portrait of a Saint . . . Warts and All*—Genesis 12–25

How to Order by Mail

Simply mark on the order form whether you want the series or individual tapes. Mail the form with your payment to the appropriate address listed below. We will process your order as promptly as we can.

United States: Mail your order to the Sales Department at Insight for Living, Post Office Box 4444, Fullerton, California 92634. If you wish your order to be shipped first-class for faster delivery, add 10 percent of the total order amount (not including California sales tax). Otherwise, please allow four to six weeks for delivery by fourth-class mail. We accept personal checks, money orders, Visa, and MasterCard in payment for materials. Unfortunately, we are unable to offer invoicing or COD orders.

Canada: Mail your order to Insight for Living Ministries, Post Office Box 2510, Vancouver, British Columbia V6B 3W7. Please add 7 percent of your total order for first-class postage and allow approximately four weeks for delivery. Our listeners in British Columbia must also add a 6 percent sales tax to the total of all tape orders (not including postage). We accept personal checks, money orders, Visa, or MasterCard in payment for materials. Unfortunately, we are unable to offer invoicing or COD orders.

Overseas: In Australia, mail your order to Insight for Living Ministries, GPO Box 2823 EE, Melbourne, Victoria 3001. Other overseas residents should contact our Fullerton office. Please allow six to ten weeks for delivery by surface mail. If you would like your order sent airmail, the delivery time may be reduced. Whether you choose surface or airmail, postage costs must be added to the amount of purchase and included with your order. Please use the following chart to determine correct postage. Due to fluctuating currency rates, we can accept only personal checks made payable in U.S. funds, international money orders, Visa, or MasterCard in payment for materials.

Type of Postage	Cassettes
Surface	10% of total order
Airmail	25% of total order

For Faster Service, Order by Telephone

To purchase using Visa or MasterCard, you are welcome to use our **toll-free** numbers between the hours of 8:30 A.M. and 4:00 P.M., Pacific time, Monday through Friday. The number to call from anywhere in the United States is **1-800-772-8888**. To order from Canada, call 1-800-663-7639. Vancouver residents should call (604) 272-5811. Telephone orders from overseas are handled through our Sales Department at (714) 870-9161. We are unable to accept collect calls.

Our Guarantee

Our cassettes are guaranteed for ninety days against faulty performance or breakage due to a defect in the tape. For best results, please be sure your tape recorder is in good operating condition and is cleaned regularly.

Note: To cover processing and handling, there is a $10 fee for *any* returned check.

Order Form

Please send me the following cassette tapes:

The current series: ☐ ABE CS Abraham . . . The Friend of God

Individual tapes:
☐ ABE 1   ☐ ABE 4   ☐ ABE 7   ☐ ABE 10
☐ ABE 2   ☐ ABE 5   ☐ ABE 8   ☐ ABE 11
☐ ABE 3   ☐ ABE 6   ☐ ABE 9   ☐ ABE 12

I am enclosing:

$ _____ To purchase the cassette series for $65.25 (in Canada $83.00*) which includes the album cover

$ _____ To purchase individual tapes at $5.00 each (in Canada $6.35*)

$ _____ Total of purchases

$ _____ If the order will be delivered in California, please add 6 percent sales tax

$ _____ U.S. residents please add 10 percent for first-class shipping and handling if desired

$ _____ *British Columbia residents please add 6 percent sales tax

$ _____ Canadian residents please add 7 percent for postage

$ _____ **Overseas residents please add appropriate postage** (See postage chart under "How to Order by Mail.")

$ _____ As a gift to the Insight for Living radio ministry for which a tax-deductible receipt will be issued

$ _____ **Total amount due (Please do not send cash.)**

Form of payment:

☐ Check or money order made payable to Insight for Living

☐ Credit card (Visa or MasterCard only)

If there is a balance: ☐ apply it as a donation   ☐ please refund

---

Credit card purchases:

☐ Visa   ☐ MasterCard Number _____

Expiration Date _____

Signature _____

We cannot process your credit card purchase without your signature.

Name _____

Address _____

_____

City _____

State/Province _____ Zip/Postal Code _____

Country _____

Telephone (____) _____ Radio Station __ __ __ __

Should questions arise concerning your order, we may need to contact you.

CCCC   ECFA MEMBER

Order Form

Please send me the following cassette tapes:

The current series: ☐ ABE CS Abraham ... The Friend of God

Individual tapes:
☐ ABE 1 ☐ ABE 4 ☐ ABE 7 ☐ ABE 10
☐ ABE 2 ☐ ABE 5 ☐ ABE 8 ☐ ABE 11
☐ ABE 3 ☐ ABE 6 ☐ ABE 9 ☐ ABE 12

I am enclosing:

$ _____ To purchase the cassette series for $65.25 (in Canada $83.00*) which includes the album cover

$ _____ To purchase individual tapes at $5.00 each (in Canada $6.35*)

$ _____ Total of purchases

$ _____ If the order will be delivered in California, please add 6 percent sales tax

$ _____ U.S. residents please add 10 percent for first-class shipping and handling if desired

$ _____ *British Columbia residents please add 6 percent sales tax

$ _____ Canadian residents please add 7 percent for postage

$ _____ **Overseas residents please add appropriate postage** (See postage chart under "How to Order by Mail.")

$ _____ As a gift to the Insight for Living radio ministry for which a tax-deductible receipt will be issued

$ _____ **Total amount due (Please do not send cash.)**

Form of payment:

☐ Check or money order made payable to Insight for Living

☐ Credit card (Visa or MasterCard only)

If there is a balance: ☐ apply it as a donation ☐ please refund

Credit card purchases:

☐ Visa ☐ MasterCard Number _____

Expiration Date _____

Signature _____

We cannot process your credit card purchase without your signature.

Name _____

Address _____

_____

City _____

State/Province _____ Zip/Postal Code _____

Country _____

Telephone ( ) _____ Radio Station __ __ __ __

Should questions arise concerning your order, we may need to contact you.

Order Form

Please send me the following cassette tapes:

The current series: ☐ ABE CS Abraham . . . The Friend of God

Individual tapes: ☐ ABE 1 ☐ ABE 4 ☐ ABE 7 ☐ ABE 10
☐ ABE 2 ☐ ABE 5 ☐ ABE 8 ☐ ABE 11
☐ ABE 3 ☐ ABE 6 ☐ ABE 9 ☐ ABE 12

I am enclosing:

$ _____ To purchase the cassette series for $65.25 (in Canada $83.00*)
which includes the album cover

$ _____ To purchase individual tapes at $5.00 each (in Canada $6.35*)

$ _____ Total of purchases

$ _____ If the order will be delivered in California, please add 6 percent
sales tax

$ _____ U.S. residents please add 10 percent for first-class shipping and
handling if desired

$ _____ *British Columbia residents please add 6 percent sales tax

$ _____ Canadian residents please add 7 percent for postage

$ _____ **Overseas residents please add appropriate postage**
(See postage chart under "How to Order by Mail.")

$ _____ As a gift to the Insight for Living radio ministry for which a tax-
deductible receipt will be issued

$ _____ **Total amount due (Please do not send cash.)**

Form of payment:

☐ Check or money order made payable to Insight for Living
☐ Credit card (Visa or MasterCard only)
If there is a balance: ☐ apply it as a donation ☐ please refund

---

Credit card purchases:
☐ Visa ☐ MasterCard Number _____
Expiration Date _____
Signature _____
We cannot process your credit card purchase without your signature.

Name _____

Address _____

_____

City _____

State/Province _____ Zip/Postal Code _____

Country _____

Telephone ( ) _____ Radio Station __ __ __ __
Should questions arise concerning your order, we may need to contact you.